THE MORAL PURPOSE
OF PROPHECY

The Harmony Between Christian Experience
and Prophetic Interpretation

Christian Realities Revealed in the
Prophetic Pictures of the Apocalypse

By Louis F. Were

THE MORAL PURPOSE OF PROPHECY

By Louis F. Were

© 2014 by Laymen Ministries/
LMN Publishing International, Inc.
ISBN: 978-0-9961896-8-2

Published by:
LAYMEN MINISTRIES
414 Zapada Rd.
St. Maries, ID 83861

The references in this edition have been carefully checked, and as a result, may differ slightly in some cases from the original text Every effort has been made to ensure that all references are accurate. Italic emphasis applied in quotes from various sources are supplied by the author.

A faithful, trusting heart is held as an impregnable fortress "upon a very high mountain" (Ezek. 40:2; 43:12; Eph. 1:3; 6:12; Rev. 14:1; etc.) in the midst of hostile foes.

The power, or "gates of hell shall not prevail against it" (Matt. 16:18).

"Kept by the power of God through faith" (1 Peter 1:5).

"Strengthened with might by His Spirit in the inner man; that Christ may dwell in your hearts by faith" (Eph. 3:16, 17).

"We [the Father, Son and Holy Spirit] will . . . make Our abode with him" (John 14:23).

"I will encamp about Mine house" (Zech. 9:8). "For I, saith the Lord, will be unto her a wall of fire round about her, and will be the glory in the midst of her" (Zech. 2:5). "Turn you to the strong hold" (Zech. 9:12).

A MIGHTY FORTRESS

A mighty fortress is our God,
A bulwark never failing;
Our Helper He amid the flood
Of mortal ills prevailing.
For still our ancient foe
Doth seek to work us woe;
His craft and power are great,
And armed with cruel hate,
On earth is not his equal.

Did we in our own strength confide,
Our striving would be losing;
Were not the right Man on our side,
The Man of God's own choosing.
Dost ask who that may be?
Christ Jesus, it is He!
Lord Sabaoth His name,
From age to age the same;
And He must win the battle.

And though this world with devils filled,
Should threaten to undo us,
We will not fear, for God hath willed
His truth to triumph through us.
Let goods and kindred go,
This mortal life also;
The body they may kill;
God's truth abideth still,
His kingdom is forever.

— Martin Luther

Contents

FOREWORD

Students of the Bible realize the vast importance of having correct views about those prophecies which still remain unfulfilled. What will the future be like? Can we know what sort of a world we shall be living in tomorrow? Or is there to be any tomorrow? So discordant are the voices of those who claim to know what the prophecies of the Bible predict, that the average man is tempted to say, with the perplexed and despairing Jewish exiles of the Babylonian captivity:—

"We see not our signs: there is no more any prophet: neither is there among us any that knoweth how long" (Ps. 74:).

But it is the part of faith to believe that God is still in His heaven, even though all is not right with the world, and to believe that He must have revealed to us in the Holy Scriptures the real truth about the world's future. How can we rightly interpret what He has given us?

The Jews of nineteen centuries ago had all that God had then revealed. And they should have understood correctly what God had foretold. Why did they make such a sad blunder about all the prophecies concerning their Messiah? And when we see great numbers of present-day Christians adopting the very same methods of interpreting the prophecies which were used by the Pharisees, how can we have any confidence that these men know what they are doing?

It is undeniable that the modern Futurists, represented by scores of Bible Institutes and by the Scofield Bible, have adopted the same extreme "literalism" which the Jews held in the time of Christ. That deluded method of interpreting prophecy sent their true Messiah to Calvary, and sent themselves into national destruction and into a second Diaspora to the four winds. How can any spiritually minded Christian follow such methods of interpretation in these days of the last crisis of mankind?

9

Every student of the subject has noticed that all the prophecies of both the Old Testament and the New are given in a distinctly Jewish or Palestinian setting. But instead of adopting a crass literalism, so utterly contrary to all of the many cases where interpretations of Old Testament prophecies have been given in the New, why not ask ourselves how any prophecies could have been given to the Jews with any but a Jewish or Palestinian setting or background? Would it not be essential that these prophecies be given in language which would seem to be intelligible to them, at least in some respects? There was really no other way, consistent with the distinctly moral or spiritual purposes for which the prophecies were given. But if we remain true to the declarations of both Christ and Paul regarding the absolute termination of all the special privileges and opportunities of the literal descendants of Abraham, we are obliged to interpret the prophecies, in spite of their Palestinian setting, in the light of the higher spiritual values brought in by the gospel since the crucifixion and resurrection of our Lord.

This little book deals with all these problems. With a profusion of texts, and with a clear insight into the fundamental principles of prophetic interpretation, Mr. Were has here given us a work which merits careful and continued study. It has not solved all the problems: it does not profess to do so. But it is pointing us in the right direction. Let us continue the study of these vital subjects until the Day dawns, and the Daystar arises never more to go down.

GEORGE McCREADY PRICE.

Loma Linda, California.

PREFACE

Salvation is taught not only in the gospels but also in the prophecies. The author has endeavoured to make clear the vitally important truth that the true interpretation of the prophecies illustrates how salvation is accomplished, and also strengthens the soul to resist sin. As the Word of God is the "seed" which, through the operation of the Holy Spirit, generates the new life (1 Peter 1:23), that life is revived and strengthened as often as the Word of God is read and received into the soul (1 Thes. 2:13). The "new man" (Col. 3:10, etc.) *lives* and *grows* "by *every* word that proceedeth out of the mouth of God" (Matt. 4:4; 1 Peter 2:2; 2 Peter 3:18).

In *purifying* the life (1 Peter 1:22) and *building* up the soul (Acts 20:32), the Saviour emphasizes the necessity of heeding *"every* word" of the Holy Scriptures (Matt. 4:4). Man's indefatigable enemy seeks to render ineffective to students of the Bible the life-giving energy contained in certain important prophecies of Holy Writ. He does this by means of erroneous interpretations.

The Saviour not only says, *"Search* the Scriptures" (John 5:39), but He also enquires: *"How* readest thou?" (Luke 10:26). By erroneous interpretations it is possible to "add unto" or "take away from" the Word of God, against which we are explicitly warned (Rev. 22:18, 19). He who studies the Scriptures in a way "approved unto God" is said to be "a workman that needeth not to be ashamed, *rightly dividing* the word of truth" (2 Tim. 2:15).

A true understanding of Bible prophecies reveals the gospel teaching that the abiding Presence of the Saviour affords protection and deliverance from hostile foes: victory is assured through the indwelling Spirit of God.

This booklet is sent forth with the prayer that God will bless its readers with a clearer understanding of the *moral* purpose of the prophecies and with the realization that Christ the King of glory reigns *in* the trusting heart and gives victory over sin. "We are more than conquerors through Him that loved us" (Rom. 8:37). "Christ *in* you the hope of glory" (Col. 1:27).

LOUIS F. WERE
Melbourne, Victoria, Australia.
3/3/49.

Chapter One

THE SCRIPTURES WERE GIVEN
TO REVEAL JESUS

Rightly understood, the prophecies are just as important and contain just as much concerning the Gospel as other portions of Scripture. God inspired the prophets to write the prophecies of Scripture in order that *by them* men might find salvation. The Bible is not a book composed of portions containing the essential facts of the Gospel and other less important parts containing the prophecies. Satan seeks to deflect the moral purpose of prophecies and, by false interpretations, robs them of their vitality.

The opening words of the Apocalypse distinctly inform us that the prophecies in this wonderful book have been given as "the Revelation of Jesus Christ" (Rev. 1:1). A study of the underlying principles upon which the Revelation is based enables us to know that *all* Bible prophecies are a "Revelation of Jesus Christ" as the Saviour of those who put their trust in Him, and the Destroyer of evil. Interpretations of prophecies which do not set forth in clearer light the Gospel of Christ are not God-inspired. Interpretations of prophecies which do not find their center in Jesus as Saviour, or as Destroyer of evil, are wrong applications of Scripture.

In the old sanctuary, and later in the temple of the Jews, only those dedicated to the holy office of the priesthood were permitted to view the wonderful glories to be seen within the sacred edifice. And only those whose lives are dedicated to God are permitted to see the inner beauties of the temple of truth. Said Jesus to the Jewish leaders: "Search the Scriptures; for in them ye think ye have eternal life: and they are they which *testify of Me*" (John 5:39, 46).

The New Testament shows how Jesus brought fulfillment to the Old Testament prophecies. In the unfolding of the Gospel, the New Testament employs 1,500 quotations of sentences and phrases from the Old Testament Scriptures. The first verse of Matthew shows one of the main reasons for the writing of the book of Matthew and the New Testament; namely, to show the fulfillment of the Old Testament prophecies in Jesus and His work of salvation. Through Jesus the fulfillment of the Old Testament prophecies is made certain (see 2 Cor. 1:20; Acts 13:27-37). The book of Matthew contains 99 *direct* references to the Old Testament Scriptures. Nine times he employed the formula, "That it might be fulfilled" (see Matt. 1:22, 23; 2:15, 17, 23, etc.), and at other times he referred to the fulfillment of the Old Testament prophecies, saying: "For thus it is written by the prophet" (Matt. 2:5); "Then was fulfilled that which was spoken by the prophet" (Matt. 27:9); "But all this was done, that the Scriptures of the prophets might be fulfilled" (Matt. 26:56); "For it is written" (Matt. 26:31, etc.). Thus Matthew illustrates the burden of the writers of the New Testament to show that Jesus' birth, life, ministry, death, resurrection, and the development of His church and her work, all fulfill the prophecies of the Old Testament.

The first words we read in Matthew's Gospel direct our minds back to the prophecies which were given to David and Abraham. While Solomon was the son who sat upon David's throne in the days immediately following the prediction, the longer and the real fulfillment is to be fulfilled by "a greater than Solomon" (Matt. 12:42). The peacefulness and the wisdom of the earlier part of Solomon's reign when people came from afar to learn of him, find their larger application in Christ. David was to have a son who would sit upon his throne (2 Sam. 7:12, 13, 16; Luke 1:32, 33). Abraham was promised a son who would be the channel of blessing. Isaac was the immediate fulfillment; but Isaac prefigured the greater fulfillment in Jesus Who, through His church, blesses the world (Gal. 3:16, 29; 4:28). The Old Testament prophecies which set forth the coming of the sons of Abraham and David are concentrated in the first verse of Matthew: "The book of the generation of Jesus Christ, the son of David, the son of Abraham." Thus, from its commencement, the New Testament takes the things of the Old Testament and applies them in connection with Christ and His work of redemption. Christ and His salvation is the central theme of the Bible, and to make plain the way of salvation was the sole purpose for which the Scriptures were written. As the sun is reflected in each of the millions of dewdrops, so Jesus, "the Light of the world," shines forth in every chapter of the Bible.

"*In every page*, whether history, or precept, or prophecy, the Old Testament Scriptures are irradiated with the glory of the Son of God. So far as it was of divine institution, *the entire system of Judaism* was a compacted prophecy of the gospel. To Christ 'give all the prophets witness' (Acts 10:43)" (*The Desire of Ages*, p. 211).

Chapter 2

THE JEWS FAILED TO STUDY THE SCRIPTURES IN THE LIGHT OF GOD'S MORAL PURPOSE. A SOLEMN WARNING FOR TODAY

The Jewish religionists were masters in the outside knowledge of the Scriptures, yet, with all their reading of the Old Testament, they did not understand the prophecies. Not only were prophecies abundantly fulfilled before their eyes, but *they themselves helped to fulfill them* and yet were too spiritually blind to recognize their fulfillment. Peter declared: "Yea, and all the prophets from Samuel and those that follow after, as many as have spoken, *have likewise foretold of these days*" (Acts 3: 24). Paul proclaimed: "And when *they* [the Jews] *had fulfilled all* that was written of Him . . . the promise which was made unto the fathers, God *hath fulfilled* the same unto us their children, in that He hath raised up Jesus again" (Acts 13:27-33).

When the Old Testament prophecies, which the Jews knew so well, being "read every Sabbath," were fulfilled so accurately, how could they be so blind to their fulfillment? — especially when they ingloriously helped to fulfill them? In Acts 13:27 we are told the reason: "For they that dwell at Jerusalem, and their rulers, *because they knew Him not, nor yet the voices of the prophets* which are read every Sabbath day, *they have fulfilled them* in condemning Him." Because they knew not Jesus — *because they were not right with God Who had sent Jesus* — they misread the prophecies of the Old Testament concerning the coming of the Messiah and the establishment of His kingdom. Had they accepted Jesus as their Lord, He would have given them freedom from sin, and with power to live a personal life of victory would have come spiritual discernment to see the moral purpose of prophecy.

One writer says: —

> "The Jewish leaders had studied the teachings of the prophets concerning the kingdom of the Messiah; but they had done this, not with a sincere desire to know the truth, but *with the purpose of finding evidence to sustain their ambitious hopes!*" (*The Desire of Ages*, p. 212).

If there had been harmony in the heart with God's purpose there would have been clarity in understanding that purpose.

Correct interpretations of prophecies relating to present and future events, when examined, will be found to harmonize with present Christian experience. The more we know of God's character and the more we become like Him, the more we are enabled *experimentally* to understand the Scriptures. "That the God of our Lord Jesus Christ, the Father of glory, may give unto you the *spirit of wisdom and revelation in the knowledge of Him*: the eyes of your understanding being enlightened" (Eph. 1:17, 18). "*Grow* in grace, *and in the knowledge* of our Lord and Saviour Jesus Christ" (2 Pet. 3:18). The more we grow in grace the greater is our knowledge of our Saviour — practical, experimental knowledge. "The soul that turns to God for its help, its support, its power, by daily, earnest prayer, will have noble aspirations, *clear perceptions of truth* and duty" (*Thoughts From the Mount of Blessing,* p. 127).

"Man shall not live by bread alone, but by every word that proceedeth out of the mouth of God" (Matt. 4:4). Our Lord quoted from Deut. 8:3, where this statement is given as the *moral* reason why God gave the manna to the children of Israel. He wanted them to apply it personally in connection with the Saviour. Had the Jews in the days of our Lord experienced in their hearts the daily renewal of manna from Heaven — were they *living* by every word of God — they would have accepted gladly the Saviour's spiritual application of the giving of the manna to Himself. (See John 6:31-66. "Many therefore of His disciples, when they had heard this, said: This is an hard saying; who can hear it? . . . From that time many of His disciples went back, and walked no more with Him.") Their lives were not in harmony with the Scriptures, therefore they did not understand them.

"The Jews Studied the Prophecies, but Without Spiritual Insight"

As the spiritual condition of a church declines, more attention is paid to the externals of religion and less to the internals — a lifeless husk instead of the living grain. Literal things which have been instituted because of their *spiritual* significance lose their *spiritual* meaning, and the service of the church degenerates into formalism: the letter is emphasized as the spirit wanes. Thus it was in the experiences of ancient Israel, and it has been repeated in the experience of the Christian church. "The Jews *lost the spiritual life* from their ceremonies, and clung to the dead forms" (*The Desire of Ages*, p. 29).

As an example of the Jews' loss of spiritual vision, notice the following extract: —

"To Moses God had said concerning His commandments, 'Thou shalt bind them for a sign upon thine hand, and they shall be as frontlets between thine eyes' (Deut. 6:8). These words have a *deep meaning.* As the Word of God is meditated upon and practiced, the whole man will be ennobled. In righteous and merciful dealing, the hands will reveal, as a signet, the principles of God's law. . . . The eyes, directed toward a noble purpose, will be clear and true. . . . But by the Jews of Christ's day all this was undiscerned. The command given to Moses was construed into a direction that the precepts of Scripture should be worn upon the person. They were accordingly written upon strips of parchment, and bound in a conspicuous manner about the head or the wrists" (Ibid. 612).

Their proud disposition to flaunt an appearance of righteousness in the eyes of their fellow men caused them to interpret the Scriptures accordingly. Had they been meek and lowly in heart, they would have discerned the *spiritual* import of Deut. 6:8.

Isaiah had prophesied: "And the glory of the Lord shall be revealed, and *all flesh shall see it together*: for the mouth of the Lord hath spoken it" (Isa. 40:5). But before the *visible* glory of

God would be manifested at the Second Advent, the *spiritual* glory of God would be revealed in the character and the life of the Lord Jesus. Had the Jews been enjoying blessed fellowship with God and understood His character they would have discerned the glory of God in the life of Jesus and would have seen that the prophet spoke of the revelation of *spiritual* glory before the *literal* glory of God should be revealed.

The Jews' need of *spiritual* vision was also illustrated by their blindness to the meaning of the prophecy in Hag. 2:7-9. Commenting upon this prophecy, the author of *The Great Controversy*, pp. 23, 24, says: —

> "This temple [Solomon's] was the most magnificent building which the world ever saw. Yet the Lord had declared, . . . 'The *glory* of this latter house shall be *greater than of the former.* . . . I will *fill* this house with *glory.*' . . . But the second temple had not equaled the first in magnificence; nor was it hallowed by those visible tokens of the divine presence which pertained to the first temple. There was no manifestation of supernatural power to mark its dedication. . . . For centuries the Jews had vainly endeavoured to show wherein the promise of God given by Haggai had been fulfilled; yet *pride and unbelief blinded their minds to the true meaning* of the prophet's words. The second temple was not honored with the cloud of Jehovah's glory, but with the living presence of One in Whom dwelt the fullness of the Godhead bodily. . . . In the presence of Christ, and *in this only*, did the second temple *exceed the first in glory.*"

Had the Jews been right with God they would have recognized the grandeur and glory of God shining out in the character of Christ; they would have thus seen the fulfillment of the prophecy of Haggai. When Jesus said: "I say unto you, That in this place is One greater than the temple" (Matt. 12:6), they would have recognized the presence of the God Whom alone they thought greater than the temple (see 2 Chron. 6:18). They would have seen the fulfillment of the prophecy of Mal. 3:1: "The Lord, whom ye seek, shall suddenly come to His temple."

Jesus also said: "The queen of the south shall rise up in the judgment with this generation, and shall condemn it: for she came from the uttermost parts of the earth to hear the wisdom of

Solomon; and, behold, *a greater than Solomon is here"* (Matt. 12:42). Had the Jews read the Old Testament history aright they would have seen that the history of notable persons such as Solomon was recorded in Scripture to typify the coming of someone greater; even the long-promised Messiah, and when Jesus made these statements they would have seen readily the glorious privilege which was theirs.

The Old Testament contains many predictions concerning the Messiah's kingdom.

"At the time . . . when our Lord appeared, there was *a general expectation among the Jews of the coming of the Messiah*, and His reign was called 'the world to come,' 'the heavenly Jerusalem,' 'the kingdom of heaven,' or 'of God.' To enter the kingdom was to become His disciple. The Jews had very erroneous conceptions of its nature; and it was necessary that our Lord should correct them. This He does in the teachings of Himself, and of His disciples. *The nature of the kingdom of God must be learned, therefore, from the New Testament"* (*Angus's Bible Handbook*, p. 203).

When the Messiah came "unto His own," "His own received Him not" (John 1:11). The Jews rejected Christ because His interpretation of the Old Testament prophecies of the expected kingdom was not what they wanted. *Their hearts were not prepared for the kind of kingdom He preached.* Says the writer already quoted: —

"Some of the Pharisees had come to Jesus demanding 'when the kingdom of God should come.' More than three years had passed since John the Baptist gave the message, that like a trumpet call had sounded through the land, 'The kingdom of heaven is at hand.' And as yet these Pharisees saw no indication of the establishment of the kingdom. Many of those who rejected John, and at every step had opposed Jesus, were insinuating that His mission had failed. Jesus answered: '*The kingdom of God cometh not with outward show*; neither shall they say, Lo here! or, Lo there! for, behold, *the kingdom of God is within you.*' *The kingdom of God begins in the heart.* Look not here or there for manifestations of earthly power to mark its coming. . . . *Because* it is *not* attended by *worldly pomp*, you are in *danger of failing to discern the glory of My mission"* (*The Desire of Ages*, p. 506).

The Jews looked forward to the time when, with the advent of the Messiah, all the predictions regarding the exaltation of Israel in His literal kingdom would have their grand fulfillment. The two-fold nature of the Messiah's kingdom their unspiritual natures could not grasp.

Not wishing to see this two-fold nature prophesied by the seers of Israel, they failed to heed the truth that the *first* phase of the kingdom had to do with humiliation and the battle against evil within. Christ had to *suffer* before He entered into *glory* (Luke 24:25, 26, 46; 1 Pet. 1:11). Similarly, the "Israel" associated with Him would likewise first suffer before they reigned in glory with Him (2 Tim. 2:12; 1 Pet. 4:13).

The proud human heart would like to share in the glory, but not in the humiliation and the suffering, which are essential for entrance into the kingdom (Acts 14:22). The first phase of the Messiah's kingdom is the kingdom of grace, during which time and opportunity are afforded for a heart preparation for the glory to follow.

"Life" is a synonym for "the kingdom of God" (Mark 9:45, 47; Matt. 18:9); in the kingdom of grace Jesus gives spiritual life. In the kingdom of glory He gives eternal life. Christ, by His Spirit, *now* reigns in every heart on earth subject to Him (Col.1:13, 26, 27; 3:4; 1 John 3:14; 5:11-13; John 3:3, 7; Phil. 3:20; Heb. l2:23, margin; Eph. 2:6, etc.). This was the kingdom which was "at hand" (Matt. 3:2; 4:17, etc.). This was the burden of Paul's sermons (see Acts 20:25; 28:23, 31). Prophecies concerning the Messiah's kingdom *are now* being fulfilled *spiritually, but one needs to have that experimental knowledge of the indwelling Spirit of Christ in order, to fully appreciate their present-day fulfillment.*

Failing to read the prophecies in the light of Christ's work of salvation caused the Jews to misunderstand the prophecies they knew so well. Unless our interpretations of prophecies reveal Christ we, too, will fail to grasp their true meaning. The Jews were led to reject Christ because of their misinterpretation of the prophecies concerning Israel: they forgot or overlooked the moral purpose of prophecy — *personal* salvation from sin. "Thou shalt call His name Jesus: for He shall save His people from their sins" (Matt. 1: 21).

Spiritual pride, selfishness and sin in their hearts beclouded their spiritual discernment.

> "While the Jews desired the advent of the Messiah, they had no true conception of His mission. *They did not seek the redemption from sin, but deliverance from the Romans.* They had studied the prophecies, but *without spiritual insight.* . . . Pride obscured their vision. They *interpreted prophecy* in accordance with their *selfish desires*" (*The Desire of Ages*, p. 30).

The Jews Were Rigid Literalists

The Jews were rigid *literalists* in the interpretation of the Scriptures. When Jesus said to Nicodemus, "Ye must be born again," Nicodemus affected to understand His words *literally*, as if Jesus referred to a physical birth. Jesus, of course, referred to a spiritual birth (see John 3). When Jesus said: "Destroy this temple, and in three days I will raise it up. Then said the Jews: Forty and six years was this temple in building, and wilt Thou rear it up in three days? *But He spake of the temple of His body*" (John 2:19-21). On the authority of the prophecy of Mal. 3:1 and 4:5 the Jews were expecting Elijah *literally* to return to the earth before the coming of the Messiah. This gave rise to the question: How could Jesus be the Messiah since Elijah had not yet appeared in person (Matt. 17:10; John 1:21)? Jesus answered the objection raised by the Pharisees by declaring that Malachi's prophecy regarding the coming of Elijah was fulfilled in the ministry of John the Baptist, that Elijah was a *type* of the Forerunner (see Matt. 17:11-13). When Jesus said: "He that eateth my flesh and drinketh my blood, hath everlasting life," He was speaking of a *spiritual* relationship in terms of an Old Testament type. Jesus' Jewish hearers, being *literalists*, misunderstood His words. The author of *The Desire of Ages,* pp. 389-391, gives the following comment upon this incident in the Saviour's earthly ministry:—

> "The same truth that was *symbolized* in the paschal service was taught in the words of Christ. But it was still undiscerned. Now the rabbis exclaimed angrily, 'How can this man give us His flesh to eat?' They affected to understand His words in the same *literal* sense as did Nicodemus when he asked, 'How can a

man be born when he is old?' . . . By misconstruing His words, they hoped to prejudice the people against Him. Christ did not soften down His *symbolical representation.* . . . The unbelieving Jews refused to see any except *the most literal meaning* in the Saviour's words. . . . They [His followers who rejected His testing, *spiritual* truths] cared not for *the mysterious spiritual kingdom* of which He spoke."

The Jews were expositors of prophecy "but without *spiritual insight*"; they did not study the prophecies in the light of God's moral purpose; they did not study the prophecies so that by them they would be strengthened to overcome sin in the heart. And yet it was for this purpose that they were given.

Chapter Three

HISTORY REPEATS ITSELF

Similarly today, many thousands of professing Christians study the prophecies and mis-apply them in the same way as did the Jews: their interpretation of the prophecies agrees with the Christ-rejecting Jews and is actually opposed to the plain teachings of the New Testament. The Jews pointed to the prophecies picturing the triumph of Israel over her foes (such as those in Ezek. 38, 39; Joel 3; Zech. 12 and 14, etc.) and felt certain of the protection and blessing of God. Today, Christian expositors teach the same as did the Jews regarding those prophecies. Both have overlooked the spiritual qualifications required by those whose victory and blessedness are depicted: both have overlooked the moral purpose of the prophecies.

In the days of our Lord, when the Jews read the promise contained in Jer. 31:31-37, they applied it unconditionally to their nation. An author, whose works give evidence of keen spiritual insight, says :—

"The Jews had misinterpreted God's promise of *eternal favor to Israel* [the words of Jer. 31:33, 34 are then quoted]. Thus saith the Lord. . . . If those ordinances [sun, moon and stars] depart from Me, saith the Lord, then the seed of Israel also shall cease from being a nation before Me forever' (Jer. 31:35-37). The Jews regarded their natural descent from Abraham as giving them a claim to this promise. *But they overlooked the conditions which God had specified.* Before giving the promise, He had said, 'I will put My law in their inward parts, and write it in their hearts. . . .'

"*To a people in whose heart His law is written, the favor of God is assured*" (*The Desire of Ages*, p. 106).

The New Testament clearly teaches that the church has inherited all the promises and blessings assured to Israel. To the Jews, Jesus said:—

"The Kingdom of God shall be taken from you [literal Israel] and given to a nation [spiritual Israel] bringing forth *the fruits thereof*" (Matt. 21:43). To those who bear the "*fruit* of the spirit" (Gal. 5:22, 23) in the Lord's vineyard (Matt. 21:33-43; John 15:1-11, etc.) are assured the blessing and protection of God. "Ye [the church] are . . . an holy nation" (1 Peter 2:9). That the church is now the nation of Israel is maintained throughout the New Testament. This fact has been emphasized by many esteemed Bible commentators. We will quote one, representing a large number of others who could be quoted:—

"*The Christian church absorbs the Jewish, inherits her privileges*, and adopts, with wider and nobler meaning, her phraseology. . . . The Israel of God, *the church of Christ, takes the place of the national Israel*" (*Ellicot's Commentary*, Notes on Revelation, pp. 96, 125).

It cannot be too strongly stressed that this statement expresses the clear and frequently repeated teaching of the New Testament, and the explicitly stated declaration of Protestant churches and commentators. But, alas! the enemy of truth has been working assiduously to blind people to the true interpretation of the Scriptures so that they will not see the moral purpose of the prophecies which is vital for them to understand in this the hour of destiny. The time-tested belief of the church, that the kingdom prophecies of the Old Testament have found their larger, moral fulfillment in the New Testament Church, is being thrust aside for a relatively new and decidedly revolutionary teaching called Dispensationalism, which declares that these prophecies "skip over" the Church age and will be literally fulfilled in a Jewish kingdom age which will follow it. This revolutionary teaching drastically revises the interpretation of the book of Revelation, and students of the Revelation should prayerfully consider as to whether their interpretation of that book is influenced by the principles of Futurism. Writing in condemnation of this system of interpretation, Dr. Oswald T. Allis points out its fundamental error:—

"Dispensationalism has its source in a faulty and unscriptural *literalism* which, in the important field of prophecy, *ignores the typical and preparatory character of the Old Testament*. . . . This Dispensational system of interpreting Scripture is very popular today. The reasons are not far to seek. *Literal* interpretation seems to make Bible study easy. It also seems reverent. It argues on this wise: 'God must have said just what He means, and must mean just what He has said; and what He has said is to be taken just as He said it, i.e., *literally*.' But the New Testament makes it plain that *literal* interpretation was a stumbling block to the Jews. It concealed from them the most precious truths of Scripture. The temple and its worship were typical of the high priestly work of Christ (John 2:19). But the Jews failed to understand His application of it to Himself, and used His words to encompass His destruction (Matt. 26:61). . . . He came to fulfill the law and the prophets. But the fulfillment which He offered the Jews was so different from their *literal* and carnal desires and expectations that they sent their King to Calvary" (*Prophecy and the Church*, pp. 256, 258).

History repeats itself. The Jews looked for an earthly and temporal dominion. They claimed the literal, unconditional fulfillment of the prophecies concerning "Israel," refusing to see that they forfeited their right to them because of their failure to meet the conditions. Because of their false interpretations of the prophecies concerning the kingdom promised to Israel, the Jews rejected Christ and His spiritual kingdom. Similarly, today, many professing Christians fall into the same error of interpreting the prophecies concerning "Israel" in a literal Palestinian sense, failing to see that the Jews, by their rejection and crucifixion of Christ, forfeited all right to them. As the *literal, Palestinian-centered* system of interpretation was *the means of the Jews' rejection of Christ* and His spiritual kingdom, so, today, the *literal, Palestinian-centered system of interpretation*—Futurism—*causes people to misunderstand and reject Christ's last-day Message concerning the last events in His spiritual kingdom of Israel.* This Message is clearly enunciated in the book of Revelation, but because it is couched in Old Testament terminology its present moral purpose is not understood by those following the Futuristic system of interpretation.

Because of the imagery pertaining to Israel so abundantly used in the book of Revelation, futurists say that it is a book largely pertaining to the literal Jew in Palestine. Failure to understand the New Testament principle that Old Testament *terminology* is now employed in a *spiritual*, worldwide sense *in connection with the church* is responsible for much theological confusion. "Israel" is the key-word which unlocks prophetic problems—especially those in the book of Revelation. Only as they relate to the church can the prophecies be fully understood. Many commentators rightly emphasize that "the symbolism of the Revelation is *wholly* and *exclusively Jewish*"; only spiritual Israelites can understand the prophecies of the Apocalypse. It is estimated that at least 550 quotations from the Old Testament are found in the book of Revelation. The following extract from *The Revelation of St. John,* by Prof. W. Milligan, D.D., pp. 27-30, illustrates what others have pointed out concerning the exclusively Jewish nature of the Revelation:—

"The Christian church, even among the Gentiles, had been grafted upon the stem of David. She had an interest in Zion and Jerusalem; she saw in Babylon the type of her enemies; she felt herself to be the *true Israel of God.* She was well acquainted with the *tabernacle and the temple*, with their *pillars* and *incense*, with their different *altars*, with the *high priest's robes*, with the seven-branched *golden candlesticks*, with the *ark* of the *testimony*, with the *hidden manna*, and with the parchment *rolls written* both within and on the back. These symbols were therefore closely adapted to her condition, and must have gone home to her with peculiar power.

"But the symbolism of the *Revelation* is *wholly and exclusively Jewish*. Even 'the crown of life' in Chap. 2:10 is not the wreath of the victor in Grecian games, but the Hebrew crown of royalty and joy—the crown of 'King Solomon, wherewith his mother crowned him in the day of his espousals, and in the gladness of his heart' (Song of Sol. 3:11). The 'white stone,' with the new name written in it, of chapter 2:17, is not suggested by the white pebble which, cast in heathen courts of justice into the ballot box, expressed the judge's acquittal of the prisoner at the bar, but in all probability by the glistering plate borne by the high priest upon his forehead. And all good commentators are agreed that the palms of chapter 7:9 are not the palms of heathen victors either in battle or the games, but the palms of the Feast of Tabernacles when, in the most joyful of all her national festivals, Israel celebrated that life of independence on which she entered when she marched from Rameses to Succoth, and exchanged her dwellings in the hot brickfields of Egypt for the free air of the wilderness, and the 'booths' which she erected in the open country. *The symbols of the Apocalypse are to be judged of with the feelings of a Jew*, and not with those of our own country or age."

After presenting other "Israel" features in the Revelation, Prof. Milligan continues:—

"If from the trumpets we turn to the bowls the following particulars claim our notice:—

1. The very mention of bowls at once connects us, not with the world, but with the *church*. The vessels so designated were not vials, but bowls or basins, broad and shallow, rather than narrow and deep. They were the gifts presented by the *princes of the twelve tribes of Israel* for the service of the *Tabernacle* (Num. 7), and they were used for offering on the golden altar of the sanctuary, the incense which had been kindled by coals from the altar in the court. They were instruments of religious service, and were peculiarly fitted, according to the law of recompense in kind, pervading the whole Apocalypse, to contain those judgments of the Almighty, which were designed ... for the faithless church. .... [The plagues, primarily, fall upon *spiritual* Babylon—the *apostate* church.]

2. A similar remark applies to the fact that, as mentioned in chapter 15:6, the angels which bear the seven last plagues come forth from the '*temple*' or innermost shrine of the *tabernacle* of the testimony in heaven, dressed as *priests* in pure white linen, and with golden girdles" (pp. 54, 55).

"The Book is absolutely steeped *in the memories*, the *incidents*, the *thoughts*, and the *language* of the *church's past*. To such an extent is this the case that it may be *doubted whether it contains a single figure not drawn from the Old Testament, or a single complete sentence not more or less built up of materials from the same source*. Nothing can convey a full and adequate impression upon the point, except the careful study of the book itself in this particular aspect of its contents" (p. 72).

And then he enumerates examples of the many persons, places, incidents, etc., associated with ancient Israel and mentioned in the Revelation. Prof. Milligan then continues:—

"The great earthquake of chapter 6 is taken from Haggai; the sun becoming black as sackcloth of hair, and the moon becoming blood of the same chapter, from Joel; the stars of heaven falling, the fig tree casting her untimely figs, the heavens departing as a scroll, in the same chapter, from Isaiah; the locusts of chapter 9 from Joel; the gathering of the vine of the earth in chapter 14 from Joel; and the treading of the wine-press in the same chapter, from Isaiah; the wings of the eagle upon which the woman is borne for protection to the wilderness are those of Deuteronomy and Isaiah, and the whole description of the New Jerusalem in chapter 21, is moulded upon Ezekiel.

"If we look at several of the larger visions, we shall have the same lesson brought home to us—that of the throne in heaven in chapter 4, having its prototype in Isaiah and Ezekiel; that of the opening of the seals in chapter 6, in Zechariah; that of the beast from the sea in chapter 13, in Daniel; that of the olive trees in chapter 11, in Zechariah; that of the measuring of the temple in chapter 21, in Ezekiel and Zechariah; that of the little book in chapter 10, in Ezekiel.

"Or, once more, if we take any single vision and examine its detail, we shall find that its various portions are often gathered out of different prophets, or different parts of the same prophet. Thus, in the very first vision of the book, that of the glorified Redeemer, in chapter 1:12-20, the golden candlesticks are taken from Exodus and Zechariah; the garment down to the foot, from Exodus and Daniel; the golden girdle, from Isaiah and Daniel; the hairs like white wool, from the same two prophets; the feet like unto burnished brass, from Ezekiel; the two-edged sword, from Isaiah and the Psalms; the countenance as the sun shineth in his strength, from Exodus; the falling of the Seer as dead at the feet of the person who appears to him, from Exodus, Isaiah, Ezekiel, and Daniel; the laying of the right hand of Jesus upon the Seer, from Daniel.

"It is impossible to enlarge without going over *every chapter, verse* and *clause* of the book, which is a *perfect mosaic of passages from the Old Testament*, at one time quoted verbally, at another referred to in distinct allusion, now taken from one scene in *Jewish history*, and now again from *two or three together.* . . . The sacred books of his people had been more than familiar to him. They had penetrated his whole being. . . . In the whole extent of sacred or religious literature there is to be found nowhere else such a *perfect fusion of the revelation given to Israel* with the mind of one who would either express *Israel's ideas*, or give utterance, by means of the *symbols supplied by Israel's history*, to the purest and most elevated thoughts of the Christian faith" (pp. 75, 76).

"If from persons, we turn to *places* the same rule is observable. Jerusalem and Mount Zion and Babylon and the Euphrates and Sodom and Egypt, *all familiar to us in the history of Israel*, play their part in order to denote the holiness and happiness of the saints, or the coming in of judgment, or the transgressors from whom the righteous must separate themselves. The battle of Har-Magedon has undoubted reference to one or the other, if not both, of the two great slaughters connected in the Old Testament with the plain of Megiddo (Judges 5: 19; Ps. 83:9; 2 Kings 23: 29). . . .

"While nothing can explain the last attack *upon the saints* as a gathering of Gog and Magog from the four corners of the earth, but the fact that these names had already been consecrated to a similar purpose in the prophecies of Ezekiel (chaps. 38, 39)" (Ibid. 72, 73).

A Commentary of the Bible, by Bishops and Other Clergy of the Anglican Church, says concerning Rev. 20: 8:—

"The terms 'Camp' and 'City' are *images borrowed* from the condition *of Israel in the wilderness*, and in the *Promised Land* (Ex. 14:19; Ps. 107:36)."

The "Hebrew" emphasis runs throughout the Apocalypse. Even to many Greek words John gives a "strong *Hebrew* coloring." Notice the following extract taken from the pen of Prof. W. Milligan, D.D.:—

"The writer *does*, then, *intentionally Hebraise*. . . . Nothing can be more decided than his statement (Ewald's) that the imitation of Hebrew idiom in the Apocalypse goes so far as to lead to many a change in Greek construction *with the view of imitating the constructions of the Hebrew tongue*" (Milligan's *The Revelation of St. John*, p. 260).

Referring to Rev. 9:11, the Professor states:—

"When we turn to the root of the Greek name Apollyon . . . we discover that it expresses the same meaning as the *Hebrew.*" Uriah

Smith, in his *Daniel and the Revelation*, p. 479 [1972 edition p. 503], in commenting upon Rev. 9:11, says: "His name. In Hebrew, 'Abaddon,' the destroyer; in Greek, 'Apollyon,' one that exterminates or destroys. Having two different names in two languages, it is evident that the *character*, rather than the name of the power, is intended to be represented. . . . As expressed in both languages, he is a destroyer."

In describing the destruction of the enemies of the church, John is careful to emphasize the symbolic "place called in the *Hebrew* tongue Armageddon" (Rev. 16:16). As the *character* of the power and not its *literal* name is expressed in the Hebrew name of Rev. 9:11, so it is because of the *character* or the *meaning* "in the *Hebrew* tongue" of the word Armageddon that it is mentioned in Rev. 16:16. The meaning of Armageddon is given by Christopher Wordsworth: "Armageddon or Harmageddon is formed of *two Hebrew words*—the one, har, signifying a mountain; the other, a cutting to pieces; and thus it means *the mountain of excision or slaughter.*"

Ellicott's Commentary states:—

"'The Greek is moulded by the Hebrew tendencies of the writer.'. . . Thus the *strong Hebrew* coloring is precisely what we should expect from one . . . *constantly talking over Messianic hopes and prophecies*" (pp. 5, 6).

"The prevalence of *Hebraic* influences noticeable in the Apocalypse might well fit in with the later date" (p. 11).

"The interpreter is too readily caught by *external resemblances*, and *pays too little heed to inner spiritual and ethical principles. . . . Of these principles the chief seem to be the following: (1) the root passages in the Old Testament prophecies must be considered*" (pp. 12, 15).

In *The New Testament in Greek, General Epistles and Revelation*, Bishop C. Wordsworth states:—

"*The diction of the Book of Revelation is more Hebraistic than that of any other portion of the New Testament. It adopts Hebrew idioms and Hebrew words. It studiously disregards the laws of Gentile Syntax, and even courts anomalies and solecisms; it Christianizes Hebrew words and sentiments, and clothes them* in an evangelical dress, and consecrates them to Christ. Thus, for instance, it never uses the Greek form Hierosoluma, but always employs the *Hebrew* Hierusalem; and by this name it never designates the literal Sion, but the *Christian church*."

By many illustrations Bishop Wordsworth shows the Hebrew setting, sentiment, etc., prevailing throughout the Revelation. He further says:—

"In a similar spirit of genuine catholicity, expanding the mind, and *spiritualizing the language of the Jewish nation*, and investing them with the light of the Gospel, the Apocalypse *designates the Universal Church* of Christ under the terms of a *Hebrew* nomenclature by the names of 'the Twelve Tribes of Israel.' Thus it extends the view of the Hebrew people, and enlarges the walls of Sion and the borders of Palestine till they embrace within their ample range the family of mankind. . . . The Apocalypse also elevates the heart and voice of the *Hebrew nation*, even to the court of the church glorified. Here the *Hebrew* language sounds in the solemn service of the heavenly ritual, in which the angelic choir sing praises to God, Amen, Hallelujah. . . . It deals in a similar way with *Hebrew* prophecy. It is characteristic of *Hebrew* prophecy to repeat the same predictions at different times. The Apocalypse proceeds on a similar plan."

Chapter Four

FUTURISM'S FUNDAMENTAL FALLACY

The book of Revelation was written for the church of Jesus Christ (see Rev. 1:11; 22:16; 2:7, 11, 29; 3:6, 13, 22, etc.), and at its close our Lord says: "*I Jesus* have sent Mine angel *to testify unto you these things in the churches*" (Rev. 22:16). Yet, despite the Lord's own statements given in the Revelation, and despite the plain teaching of the New Testament that the church is now "the Israel of God" (Gal. 6:16, etc.), Futurists declare that because it contains so much imagery pertaining to "Israel" it deals mainly with the literal Jew in Palestine!

To rightly appreciate any teaching it is always necessary to observe carefully its basic principles. We will let Dr. Scofield's Bible (which speaks for Futurism) state the underlying principle of Futurism: Futurism denies "*that the church is the true Israel, and that the Old Testament foreview of the kingdom is fulfilled in the church*" (p. 989).

This is, as we have shown, the direct contradiction of the plain teaching of the New Testament, and also the time-tested teaching of the Christian church for hundreds of years. Futurists ignore the plain declarations of Scripture that "wrath is come upon them [the *literal* nation of Israel] to the uttermost" (1 Thess. 2:16); that as a nation they have been so broken that they "*cannot be made whole again*" (Jer. 19:11); and that Christ had explicitly declared to them: "The Kingdom of God shall be *taken from you*, and given to a nation [the church, 1 Peter 2:9] bringing forth the fruit thereof" (Matt. 21:43).

Futurists, not guided by the New Testament teaching that spiritual Israel—the church—has taken the place of national Israel, still build their doctrines and their hopes for the world upon a belief in a *literal, Palestinian fulfillment of the prophecies pertaining to Israel.* Thus Scofield's Bible, on p. 1226, comments: "The promise of the kingdom to David and his seed, described in the prophets (2 Sam. 7:8-17, refs.; Zech. 12:8) *enters the New Testament absolutely unchanged* (Luke 1:31-33)" (*italics mine*). But Scofield overlooks the fact that, as the church inherits all that belonged to Israel (in a higher sense), it also *inherits the phraseology of national Israel: the same words and designations refer to both.* In other publications the writer has given scores of examples taken from the New Testament. There is *no change in the phraseology employed in the New Testament,* but there is positively *a change regarding the people* to whom those prophecies and designations now apply. In the New Testament, the church is spoken of in the language employed in the Old Testament concerning Israel. The prophecies and blessings which at one time referred to national Israel now refer to the church. Because the church and her enemies are thus described in the Revelation, Futurists see only the literal Jewish nation and Palestine in the many references to the things of Israel contained in the book of Revelation. The Revelation can be rightly understood, its moral purpose discerned, only when Old Testament historical events, persons, names, numbers, colors, etc., are applied *spiritually* in connection with Christ and His church.

Similar to Jewish theology in the days of Jesus, Futurism is based upon a rigid, *literal* interpretation of Scripture. Concerning this Futuristic position, Dr. O. T. Allis says:—

"It is the insistent claim of its advocates that, only when interpreted literally, is the Bible interpreted truly; and they denounce as 'spiritualizers' or 'allegorizers' those who do not interpret the Bible with the same degree of literalness as they do. . . . The question of literal versus figurative interpretation is, therefore, one which has to be faced at the very outset. And it is to be observed at once that the issue cannot be stated as a simple alternative, either literal or figurative. No literalist, however thoroughgoing, takes everything in the Bible literally. Nor do those who lean to a more figurative method of interpretation, insist that everything is figurative. Both principles have their proper place and their necessary limitations. . . . The most precious teachings of the Bible are spiritual; and these spiritual and heavenly realities are often set forth under the form of earthly objects and human relationships. . . . And spiritual things are more real and more precious than visible, tangible, ephemeral things. For 'The things represented have much more of reality and perfection in them than the things by which we represent them.' The words 'This is My body' do not lose, but gain, in meaning when the literal sense is rejected as unscriptural" (*Prophecy and the Church*, pp. 16-18).

Chapter Five

FURTHER FUTURISTIC FALLACIES

Adherence to the principle that prophecies which are couched in terminology pertaining to "Israel" must be fulfilled *literally* in relation to the literal Jews postpones fulfillment to some time in the future. Thus Futurists, because these prophecies cannot be regarded as having yet been fulfilled or as being capable of fulfillment in this present age, refer their fulfillment after the "rapture" of the church. It is beyond the scope of this necessarily limited outline to discuss the subject in its many details. However, we point out that Futurists teach that Jewish peculiarities will be revived: animal sacrifices will again be offered. Scofield has endeavoured to solve the difficulty confronted by numerous New Testament texts which explicitly teach that the Mosaic ritual of sacrifices and the Aaronic priesthood have been abolished, and that the Old Testament typical system of expiation finds its fulfillment in the high priestly atonement and mediation of the Lord Jesus Christ. Scofield says: "Doubtless these offerings will be memorial, looking back to the cross, as the offerings under the old covenant were anticipatory, looking forward to the cross" (p. 890). In this, as in so many other illustrations that could be given, we see the sad result of following a system of interpretation which demands that the things pertaining to "Israel" must be *literally* fulfilled.

It is a sufficiently damning indictment of Futurism that it relegates to the future the fulfillment of such prophecies as Zech. 13:1 ("In that day there shall be a fountain opened to the house of David, and to the inhabitants of Jerusalem for sin and uncleanness"), and Dan. 9:24. The Futuristic comment is: *"The day is yet future* when a fountain shall be opened for the iniquity of Daniel's people (Zech. 13:1), and righteousness shall be ushered in for them."

It is a principle employed by Bible prophets to speak of worldwide events in the language which, at first glance, seems to indicate that Palestine is to be the place of fulfillment. But a closer study reveals that the *whole story of salvation* is couched in similar phraseology. Thus the whole of the literal local things in the Mosaic economy foreshadowed worldwide events in connection with the Christian church (see 1 Cor. 10:6, 11, margins). This has been the belief of Protestant interpreters for hundreds of years, as may be seen in the headings of the King James' Version. Though couched in phraseology indicating that the fountain for cleansing would be literally in Jerusalem, yet most Christians have applied this verse as referring to the crimson stream which has flowed from the Saviour by His death on Calvary. We may all *symbolically*, or by faith, plunge into that precious fountain wherever we are literally located on earth. Cowper's familiar hymn, "There is a Fountain Filled with Blood," owes its beautiful though painful imagery to this verse. Comparing Zech. 14:8 and Ezek. 47:1-12, we see the thought in Zech. 13:1 that water is the symbol of cleansing and purification (see also Ezek. 36:25; Rev. 7:14, etc.). The refusal to see the symbolical import of the Scriptures employed by the Holy Spirit to convey spiritual truths is the foundation of the errors of Roman Catholicism.

Chapter Six

FUTURISM AND THE BOOK OF REVELATION

As did the Jews, so do Futurists—they fail to discern the present moral purpose of the prophecies pertaining to "Israel." Old Testament terminology is employed in the Revelation *because* the church *has* taken the place of Israel; because the church *is* "Israel." God had a moral reason for giving Jacob the name "Israel"—because his character was changed after a night of prayer (see Gen. 32:24-30; Hosea 12:3, 4). Jesus is "the King of Israel" (see John 1:49). And "the King of Israel," Who knows His children, said to Nathaniel (who had spent some time with His God in prayer in the secrecy of an overhanging fig tree): "Behold *an Israelite indeed*, in whom is *no guile*" (John 1:47-49). "The remnant of Israel" (Zeph. 3:13) will be those of whom it is said: "In their mouth was found *no guile*" (Rev. 14:5). A true Israelite (like Jacob and Nathaniel, etc.) knows from experience what it means to pour out the soul before God, clinging to Him and trusting in His love and mercy. Only those who thus commune with God and who have "no guile" can fully understand or accept Christ's Message in the Revelation. The Revelation can be understood only in the light of the literal types of ancient Israel. As this principle is rejected by Futurists they cannot understand the present moral purpose of most of the prophecies of the Apocalypse. They apply them literally in connection with the literal Jew in Palestine. As nothing has yet happened literally according to their interpretation of these things of "Israel," therefore, they say, these things must be future. Thus reasoned the Jews in Christ's day and rejected Him. In this same way Futurists are blind to the present-day fulfillment of the Apocalyptic prophecies and reject Christ's vital Message for them today.

The Futuristic conception declares that Antichrist and the prophecies relating to his making "*war*" on the "saints" deal with a person who is yet to arise and do his deadly work against the *literal* Jews in Palestine. The Futuristic system of interpretation has been fostered by the Papacy because it points to a *military* Antichrist—a *literal* person—to arise in Palestine in the future, and thus diverts attention from seeing the Papacy as the Antichrist—a *spiritual* organization—portrayed in the Revelation.

The question of whether "Armageddon" is employed in a literal or a symbolic sense brings us to the decision as to the system of interpretation we employ. Futurism teaches that all Jewish matters in the Revelation are to be taken *literally*— including the "place called in the *Hebrew* tongue Armageddon." "Armageddon," they say, is a literal military battle, during which the Lord delivers the literal Jewish remnant in Palestine from their national enemies led by the beast and the false prophet. When "Armageddon" is interpreted according to the principle laid down in the New Testament, namely, that the church is now the Israel of God, "Armageddon" is seen to be a spiritual conflict involving the church and the moral principles she represents. When taught as a military battle the prophetic description of "Armageddon" has no moral purpose; when taught in relation to the destruction of the enemies of the church and the triumph of the church, it contains a vital moral purpose.

God's solemn warning against worshipping the "beast" and "his image" or receiving his "mark," as well as so many of the startling prophecies in the Revelation, lose their moral purpose for today when interpreted according to the Futuristic system, which applies them to the future in relation to the literal Jews in Palestine. Those who read these prophecies according to Futurism do so as spectators, or as those whose mental curiosity is stimulated to know what events will occur to other people who will live in Palestine in the future. But the Lord gave these prophecies as vital Messages for His true Israelites living today.

Chapter Seven

PENTECOST BROUGHT LIGHT
ON THE
MORAL PURPOSE OF PROPHECY

Even the disciples were slow to appreciate their Master's interpretation of the Old Testament kingdom prophecies. They, too, were looking for temporal deliverance from the Roman yoke, and thus they were not prepared for their terrible disappointment when they saw their Lord crucified. One writer states: —

"Before His crucifixion, the Saviour explained to His disciples that He was about to be put to death, and to rise again from the tomb. . . . But *the disciples were looking for temporal deliverance from the Roman yoke.* . . . The words which they needed to remember were banished from their minds, and when the time of trial came, it found them unprepared. The death of Jesus as fully destroyed their hopes as if He had not forewarned them" (*The Great Controversy*, p. 594).

Had the disciples a correct understanding of the prophecies they could have had a praise service in recognition of the marvelous fulfillment of prophecy in the death and resurrection of their Lord. Even on the day of the resurrection the disciples did not know the true interpretation of the prophecies concerning Israel. Before Jesus revealed Himself to the two disciples of Emmaus, He explained the prophecies, for "*it was necessary for them to understand the witness borne to Him by the types and prophecies of the Old Testament. Upon these their faith must be established.* Christ performed no miracle to convince them, but it was His first work to explain the Scriptures. They had looked upon His death as the destruction of all their hopes. Now He showed from the prophets that this was the very strongest evidence for their faith. . . . The miracles of Christ are a strong proof of His divinity; but a stronger proof that He is the world's Redeemer is found in *comparing the prophecies of the Old Testament with the history of the New*" (*The Desire of Ages*, p. 799).

Old ideas die hard, and even subsequent to the resurrection the disciples still held erroneous views regarding the fulfillment of the prophecies concerning the establishment of Christ's kingdom (Acts 1:6). Jesus had commanded them to preach: "The kingdom of heaven is at hand" (Matt. 10:7). But not until the time of Pentecost, not until they had spent weeks in prayer and the putting away of those things which were not in harmony with Christ, did the disciples really grasp the moral purpose of the prophecies.

"Just before leaving His disciples, Christ once more plainly stated the nature of His kingdom. *He recalled to their remembrance things He had previously told them regarding it.* He declared that it was *not His purpose* to establish in this world a *temporal* kingdom" (*The Acts of the Apostles*, p. 30).

"*Because of their selfishness and earthliness*, even the disciples of Jesus could not comprehend the *spiritual glory*, which He sought to reveal unto them. *It was not until after Christ's ascension* to His Father, and the outpouring of the Holy Spirit upon the believers, *that the disciples fully appreciated the Saviour's character and mission*" (*The Desire of Ages*, p. 506).

Not until the outpouring of the Holy Spirit did the disciples understand the spiritual interpretation of Old Testament prophecies regarding the kingdom. After Pentecost, while teaching a literal, physical salvation of the *future*, they also taught that *spiritual* salvation was a *present blessing* (see 1 Pet. 1:5; 1 Thess. 5:8; Rom. 13:11; Heb. 9:28; Isa. 25:9, etc.). The disciples could not, at first, see "the spiritual glory" of Christ's work fulfilling the Old Testament predictions "*because* of their *selfishness and earthliness*."

Chapter Eight

JESUS IS REIGNING NOW!

The Scriptures make it plain that the prophecies concerning the reign of David's Son were to be fulfilled by His death and resurrection (see Acts 2:29, 32; 13:22-24, 32-34; Rom. 1:3, 4; 2 Tim. 2:8). Paul preached the kingdom of God and of Christ as a then reality, into which every believer of the gospel was, and is, instantly translated (Col. 1:12, 13; 1 Cor. 15:11; Acts 20:24, 25, etc.). God has "raised unto Israel a Saviour, Jesus" (Acts 13:22, 23; Luke 2:10, 11, 30-32, 68-70; Acts 5:30, 31). By the work of the Holy Spirit in Messiah's spiritual kingdom of grace, Christ is *now* saving, redeeming Israel out of "all people" (Luke 2:30-32, etc.). That salvation is "in Zion" (Joel 2:32; Rom. 11:26; 9:33; 1 Pet. 2:4-7), the church, where Jesus reigns.

When the disciples, who were still thinking of the immediate *literal* fulfillment of the Old Testament kingdom prophecies, asked "Lord, wilt thou at this time restore again the kingdom to Israel? He said unto them, It is not for you to know the times or the seasons, which the Father hath put in His own power. *BUT ye shall receive power*, after that the Holy Ghost is come upon you" (Acts 1:6-8). The literal kingdom will be set up after the gospel age is finished at the Second Advent, and the time for that event is hidden from man, BUT the fulfillment of the prophecies concerning the Messiah's kingdom are *now* being fulfilled *through the power of the Holy Ghost.* "For the *kingdom* of God is not in word, *but in power*" (1 Cor. 4:20).

Jesus is *now* reigning! The prophecies concerning the Messiah's kingdom are *now* being fulfilled! This was the thrilling burden of the apostles' preaching after the descent of the Holy

Spirit on Pentecost! It was this recognition of the fulfillment of the kingdom prophecies in relation to the church that gave power to their preaching, and which also aroused the anger of the Jews against them. That which the Jews regarded as being wholly *future*, and to be fulfilled *literally* in connection with national Israel, the apostles preached as being fulfilled in the work of preaching the gospel. A study of the New Testament—of sermons recorded therein, or of epistles, etc., written after Pentecost—will clearly reveal this fact.

On the day of Pentecost, the inspired Peter declared that Jesus was raised to sit upon a throne; that He was "both *Lord and Christ*" (see Acts 2:30-36). Peter's sermon was very largely made up of quotations from the Old Testament. The first of these is from Joel (2:28-32), and Peter quotes these verses addressed to ancient Israel and applies them to all those who would believe in Jesus as "both Lord and Christ": "*all* flesh," "*whosoever* shall call on the name of the Lord shall be saved." In His commission to the Disciples, Jesus said: '*All power* is given unto Me in heaven and in earth. Go ye *therefore* and teach all nations" (Matt. 28:18). Thus the risen Lord spoke as a king who is about to receive His kingdom, and to take His place at the right hand of the Majesty on high. Peter in Acts 2:33 describes the outpouring of the Spirit predicted by Joel as a demonstration of the fact that He has already received and is *now exercising that royal authority*. This can only mean that Jesus had entered into His kingdom, and that this great inaugural event of the church age is to be regarded as the fulfillment of Messianic prophecy. The *King* is *now* exercising *His sovereign power*. Note this significance in such verses as Acts 3:16; 4:10, 30; 5:31, etc.

Peter quoted from Ps. 110:1: "The Lord said unto my Lord, Sit Thou at My right hand, until I make Thine enemies Thy footstool. The Lord shall send the rod of Thy strength out of Zion: *rule Thou in the midst of Thine enemies*." Jesus is *now* reigning "in the midst" of His "enemies." Peter's quotation from Joel 2:32 (see Acts 2:21 and compare with Joel 2:32) also shows that from the time of Pentecost Old Testament prophecies concerning Zion, Jerusalem, the land of Israel, etc., *were interpreted as being fulfilled in connection with the work of Christ in the gospel.* As Jesus reigns in the church, His spiritual Zion or Jerusalem, those who are pictured in Joel's prophecy (see Joel 3) as being gathered outside in the valley of Jehoshaphat to make war upon God's people within Jerusalem must refer to those who oppose the work of the gospel. This interpretation placed the Jews not as those favored of God within Jerusalem, but among those on the outside among the enemies of God. Such an interpretation aroused the anger of the Jews, who believed those prophecies would be fulfilled literally in connection with the literal nation of the Jews.

Chapter Nine

ALL SCRIPTURES ARE VIBRANT MORAL MESSAGES FROM A LIVING SAVIOUR

At Pentecost the disciples of Jesus were united in Peter's interpretation because he made his declaration "standing up *with the eleven*" (Acts 2:14). Their *present spiritual* application of the kingdom prophecies (which the Jews applied only in a strictly literal sense in relation to the future) made the Old Testament a new and a living book for them and their hearers. No longer was it a book containing dry records of the past, and future blessings which were unrelated to the present, but a Book containing a past and a future *which lived in the present*—a living book vibrant with messages from a living Christ. Not only were proofs afforded by the Old Testament itself, but *the living Christ* by his ever-present Spirit *gave an experience in harmony with the interpretation.*

The New Testament teaching is clear that, since the rejection of the Jewish nation, the church is now the "temple" in which Christ by His Spirit reigns. "The man of sin"—the counterfeit king—who was to sit "*in the temple of God*, showing himself that he is God" (2 Thess. 2:3, 4) is the Papacy within the *spiritual* temple—the professedly Christian church. Futurists—whether Papal or supposedly-Protestant—apply this prophecy in connection with a literal temple yet to be built in literal Jerusalem by an enemy of the literal Jews. Futurism fails to see the moral purpose of the prophecies concerning "the temple of God" referred to in 2 Thess. 2:3, 4, and in other temple prophecies such as described in Ezek. 40-48 and in Rev. 11:1. By applying these prophecies literally in relation to the future and Palestine, they fail to understand the *present* moral purpose for which they were given.

Paul not only spoke of the church as being God's "temple," but also of each individual (Ephes. 2:21, 22; 1 Cor. 3:16, 17; 6:19, etc.). The tabernacle in the wilderness was made after the heavenly "pattern" (Ex. 25:9, 40). After Moses had completed every detail of the structure and all the furnishings "as the Lord had commanded" him (Ex. 40:16, 19, 21, 23, 25, 27, 29, 31), "the glory of the Lord *filled* the tabernacle" (v. 35). The same thing occurred at the dedication of Solomon's temple (1 Kings 8:10, 12; 2 Chron. 5:13, 14; 7:2). The spiritual lesson is obvious: when we do all that the Lord commands us to do we, too, shall be *filled* with the glory of God. The New Testament command: "Be *filled* with the Spirit" (Ephes. 5:18) is tantamount to urging us to obey God in everything, for only in this way will the Spirit of God flood the soul with His glory. ". . . the Holy Ghost, *Whom God hath given to them that obey Him*" (Acts 5:32).

The temple described so minutely in Ezek. 40-48 also has its present fulfillment in the Christian church, and each individual believer. Individually as well as collectively the Messiah is now building His "temple" in which He now reigns in power (Zech. 6:12, 15; 1 Cor. 3:16, 17; 6:19; Ephes. 2:21, 22, etc.). The minute and most exact measurements of each part of the temple is experienced by those who seek to do only that which is in harmony with the Divine measuring rod (compare Ezek. 40:3, etc., with Rev. 11:1). Christian experience harmonizes with the interpretation. All the temple scenes of the Bible—whether as recorded in the history of ancient Israel or in the prophetic portions of Scripture—were written to typify God's moral purpose, and that by them individuals might find the way of salvation. This truth has been clearly pointed out by the author of the book entitled: *The Desire of Ages*. This well-known writer says: —

> "From eternal ages it was *God's purpose* that every created being, from the bright and holy seraph to man, *should be a temple for the indwelling of the Creator*. Because of sin, humanity ceased to be a temple for God. . . . But by the incarnation of the

Son of God, the purpose of Heaven is fulfilled. *God dwells in humanity,* and through saving grace the heart of *man becomes again His temple.* God designed that the temple at Jerusalem *should be a continual witness to the high destiny open to every soul"* (p. 161).

"In the cleansing of the temple, Jesus was announcing His mission as the Messiah, and entering upon His work. . . . *In cleansing the temple* from the world's buyers and sellers, Jesus announced His mission to *cleanse the heart* from the defilement of sin—from the earthly desires, the selfish lusts, the evil habits, that corrupt the soul" (ibid.).

Solomon's magnificent temple symbolized the church and each believer. Concerning the building of this temple on Mount Moriah we read: "And the house, when it was in building, was built of stone made ready before it was brought thither: so that *there was neither hammer nor axe nor any tool of iron heard* in the house, while it was in building" (1 Kings 6:7). The noiseless building of this temple typified the building of Christ's spiritual temple by the quiet operations of the Spirit of God (see Ephes. 2:21, 22). The author of *"Prophets and Kings,"* p. 36, says:—

"Of surpassing beauty and unrivalled splendor was the palatial building which Solomon and his associates erected for God and His worship. Garnished with precious stones . . . was *a fit emblem of the living church of God on earth*, which through the ages has been building in accordance with the divine pattern, with materials that have been likened to 'gold, silver, precious stones,' 'polished after the similitude of a palace' (1 Cor. 3:12; Ps. 144:12). Of this *spiritual* temple Christ is 'the chief cornerstone; in Whom all the building fitly framed together groweth unto an holy temple in the Lord.'"

"Through Christ was to be fulfilled *the purpose of which the tabernacle was a symbol*—that glorious building, its walls of glistening gold reflecting in rainbow hues the curtains in wrought with cherubim, the fragrance of ever-burning incense pervading all, the priests robed in spotless white, and in the deep mystery of the inner place, above the mercy seat, between the figures of the bowed, worshipping angels, the glory of the Holiest. *In all, God desired His people to read His purpose for the human soul"* (*Education*, p. 36).

"Though the ministration was to be removed from the earthly to the heavenly temple; though the sanctuary and our great High Priest would be invisible to human sight, yet the disciples were to suffer no less thereby. . . . While Jesus ministers in the sanctuary above, *He is still by His Spirit the minister of the church on earth*" (*The Desire of Ages*, p. 166).

"We are in the day of atonement, and we are to work in harmony with Christ's work of *cleansing the sanctuary from the sins of the people.* . . . Those who do not sympathize with Jesus in His work in the heavenly courts, who do not *cleanse the soul temple* of every defilement . . . are joining with the enemy of God and man" (*Review and Herald*, January 21, 1890).

"*His church is to be a temple* built after the divine similitude, and the angelic architect has brought his golden measuring rod from heaven, that every stone may be hewed and squared by the divine measurement, and polished to shine as an emblem of heaven, radiating in all directions the bright, clear beams of the Sun of Righteousness" (*Testimonies to Ministers*, p. 17).

In these extracts we see applied the principle that the tabernacle in the wilderness, the temple in Jerusalem, and the temple described in prophecy, symbolized God's moral purpose for His church and for each individual.

Incidents, such as the Babylonians' destruction of Solomon's temple (2 Chron. 36:17-19); their carrying off to Babylon the vessels belonging to the house of God (2 Chron. 36:18; Ezra 1:7-11; Dan. 1:2) and using them there in the service of their false gods (Dan. 5:2, 3); the deliverance and the return of ancient Israel from their Babylonian captivity, the rebuilding of the broken down temple and city of Jerusalem, etc., *are all recorded in the Scriptures* (Ezra, Neh., Hag., etc.) *for a moral purpose.* While the study of sacred history is interesting and profitable in itself, yet the main reason for which these incidents are recorded is that by them we might receive spiritual strength. "For *whatsoever things were written aforetime were written for our learning,* that we through patience and comfort of the Scriptures might have hope" (Rom. 15:4). Not only may we discern the building of Christ's church and of each individual believer *in the building of the tabernacle and the temple,* but the *restoration* of the backslidden soul or church as an habitation of

God may be seen in the *rebuilding and restoration* of the temple and its services after being subjected to assault and damage at the hand of the forces of Babylon. A writer who always draws the moral lesson from the historical records of Scripture, says:—

> "The work of *restoration* and reform carried on by the returned exiles, under the leadership of Zerubbabel, Ezra, and Nehemiah, presents a picture of a work of *spiritual restoration* that is to be wrought in the closing days of this earth's history. . . . Varied were the experiences that came to them as they *rebuilt the temple* and the wall of Jerusalem; strong was the opposition they had to meet. . . . The *spiritual restoration* of which the work carried forward in Nehemiah's day was a *symbol*, is outlined in the words of Isaiah: 'They shall build the old wastes, they shall raise up the former desolations, and they shall repair the waste cities' (Isa. 61:4). 'They that shall be of thee shall build the old waste places: thou shalt raise up the foundations of many generations; and thou shalt be called, The repairer of the breach, The restorer of paths to dwell in' (Isa. 58:12)" (*Prophets and Kings*, p. 677).

When describing the call of God's people out of spiritual Babylon, the Revelator (he uses the same principle throughout the Apocalypse), refers to the moral purpose of literal Israel's call out of the literal city of Babylon, and their return to Jerusalem to rebuild the temple and city (see Rev. 18:4). Individually, people are now being called out of Babylon to repair and to restore the true worship of God.

The damage done in the Dark Ages by the spiritual Babylonians to the spiritual temple and city of God (Rev. 11:1, 2) is being repaired. The vessels taken from the house of God in Jerusalem (Dan. 1:2) and used in the service of Satan's Babylonian false system of worship (Dan. 1:2; 5:1-4) are being restored to the house of true worship (Ezra 1:1-11; Matt. 17:11). The rebuilding and restoration of an individual and the church as a temple of God are illustrated in this experience of Israel.

Keeping in mind the New Testament principle of applying Old Testament history and prophecy in connection with God's moral purpose not only causes the book to be a living book, pulsating with power and purpose, but guides us in our interpretation of prophecy.

Chapter Ten

THE INDIVIDUAL APPLICATION
OF HISTORY AND PROPHECY

The New Testament interpretation of the Old Testament prophecies concerning the kingdom and work of the Messiah is that they apply *individually as well as collectively* to the church. It is important that the individual application of prophecy be considered. All Bible prophecies center in Jesus, and they, when rightly understood, will have a bearing upon individuals. God deals with individuals: "whosoever" (John 3:16; Rev. 22:17). The Ten Commandments are written in the singular number. The promises are "to *him* that overcometh" (Rev. 2:7, 11, 17, 26; 3:5, 12, 21). Jesus says: "*He* that hath ears to hear, let *him* hear" (Matt. 11:15). Eight times in the Revelation Jesus also appeals to the individual: "He that hath an ear, let him hear" (Rev. 2:7, 11, 17, 29; 3:6, 13, 22; 13:9). The acceptance of Christ is a personal matter. The writing of the Law of God in the heart is an individual work (2 Cor. 3:3; Ps. 40:8; Ezek. 11:19, 20; 36: 26; Heb. 8:8-13).

The deliverance of Israel from Egyptian bondage not only typifies the deliverance of the church, but of the individual from the bondage of sin. The safe passage of the nation of Israel through the waters of the Red Sea (1 Cor. 10:1, 2, 11); the Israelites partaking of the manna and drinking the water from the rock (1 Cor. 10:3, 4, 11); the march of national Israel across the wilderness to the promised land (1 Pet. 2:11); the sanctuary in the midst of the camp of Israel (John 1:14, R.V.); the daily services of the sanctuary (Heb. 13:10-15; Rom. 12:1, etc.); the cleansing of the sanctuary (1 John 1:9, etc.); the writing of the Law of God upon two tables of stone (1 Cor. 3:3); the temple (John 2:21; 1 Cor. 3:19); the kings and the priests of Israel (Rev. 1:6; 5:10; 20:6), etc., are, in the New Testament, applied in connection with the individual believer, as well as to the church as a whole. In this way the Lord has shown us that our interpretation of the contents of Scripture, whether of the history of past events in the experiences of God's people, or concerning prophecies of the future, should have a *present* message for the individual. In this way the Book is vibrant with a living message of power and authority; in this way we also learn to test interpretations of prophecy.

Blessings which are stated in the Word of God to be the future inheritance of the saints are applicable to the believer today. Thus Paul quotes from Isa. 64:4, and applies the promises of future things as belonging to the present: "Eye hath not seen, nor ear heard, neither have entered into the heart of man, the things which God hath prepared for them that love Him. BUT GOD HATH REVEALED THEM UNTO US BY HIS SPIRIT" (1 Cor. 2:9, 10). "Behold, I make all things new" (Rev. 21:5) is God's promise concerning the eternal kingdom. "Behold, all things *are* become new" (2 Cor. 5:17), declared Paul of those "in Christ." Elsewhere, the writer has shown by a number of examples that future blessings are applied as present spiritual realities to those who are "in Christ." As the past events of Israel are applied in the New Testament in relation to present experiences of individuals and of the church (1 Cor. 10:6, 11, margins), and that which is future is also thus applied, the Bible is therefore a book alive with messages for the present. The past and the future become *present realities*. Today's experiences will harmonize with the experiences recorded in the history of God's ancient people and also harmonize with what is revealed regarding the future kingdom of glory. The present life of the Christian is not something entirely different from the experiences of Israel; it is not something entirely foreign to future experiences and events in God's kingdom of glory.

With these guiding principles before us in our study of the Bible it becomes a living book which is vibrant with meaning concerning Christ and each individual believer. In the inspired record of creation we may see also the work of the Holy Spirit upon our unshaped characters; calling order out of chaos; light instead of darkness, etc. In the record of the flood we may also see our rescue by the means of the ark God has provided. The deliverance of the Israelites from Egypt foreshadows our deliverance from sin. Pharaoh's endeavor to keep God's people in bondage illustrates how Satan endeavors to hold us in his grasp. As we seek to serve God, Satan seeks to make the way harder, just as Pharaoh made the lot of Israel more difficult. When we flee from Egypt, Satan pursues us to slay us or to again take us captive. Our faith is tested at the Red Sea. God opens up a way of escape for us from our foes. We come to the bitter waters which are made sweet only by the Branch (Christ) (Zech. 6:12, etc.). We, too, are fed by the heavenly manna, which must be eaten each day; drink of the water of life gushing from the Smitten Rock (1 Cor. 10:1-4); bitten by serpents but cured by looking to Christ (John 3:14, etc.); attacked by enemies as we journey to the promised land; overcome our foes as our great Leader pleads for us on high; have a foretaste of the fruits of coming inheritance; cross over Jordan's cold billows and enter in triumph into Canaan.

In the sanctuary and its services we see clear and definite *illustrations* of the various features connected with the plan of redemption. An innocent, unblemished lamb slain because of an individual's sin presents an impressive picture of Christ's substitutionary death. The word picture of the Israelites sheltering behind the blood-sprinkled door lintels while the death angel passes by, graphically portrays the effectiveness of the blood of Jesus to save us from God's wrath against sin. By the pictures presented in the sacred narratives of the physical exploits of Samson, we see clearly illustrations of the power of the Holy Spirit in our lives, overcoming the difficulties and dangers from our spiritual foes (see Dan. 11:32; Ephes. 6:10). David's victorious conflict with Goliath provides us with a clear picture of what it means to live the victorious life in the power of Christ. Satan, our Goliath, is far too strong for us to slay, but with Paul we can say: "I can do all things through Christ which strengtheneth me" (Phil. 4:13). We obtain "the *victory* through our Lord Jesus Christ" (1 Cor. 15:57).

The historical incidents recorded in the Old Testament provide us with *word pictures* by which God teaches us spiritual truths. In them we are to see things worldwide in scope: corresponding likenesses in the spiritual realm, which are "spiritually discerned" (1 Cor. 2:14).

The New Testament reveals the principle of "spiritually" discerning "spiritual things" in the historical narratives of the Old Testament. In this way "God *hath* revealed them unto us" —the things which He "hath prepared for them that love Him." The natural eye does not discern these "spiritual things," and often interprets *literally* that which should be "spiritually discerned" (see 1 Cor. 2:6-16).

A well-known author says:—

"Undoubtedly our natural bias is in favor of the so-called 'literal' interpretation of the prophecies in question; for to the natural man the things that are seen are the *real* things; and to that view we are disposed to cling tenaciously, notwithstanding the plain teaching of the New Testament, that the seen things are fleeting shadows of things unseen, the latter being the spiritual and eternal realities with which the promises of future blessing have mainly to do. . . . Evidently, then, our difficulty in understanding prophecies of the class referred to above is due to our lack of faith and our spiritual dullness" (*The Hope of Israel*, pp. 15, 17, by P. Mauro).

The Jews, still clinging tenaciously to the belief that the prophecies concerning Israel must be *literally* fulfilled through the Jewish nation, were so blinded that they did not recognize the fulfillment of those prophecies in the experiences of the Messiah and spiritual Israel. They failed to remember that those prophecies were for those who *experienced in their lives the things portrayed in the prophetic word*. Similarly, today, modern theologians are so blinded by the belief of a literal Palestinian fulfillment of the ancient prophecies given to Israel, that they do not recognize the spiritual fulfillment *now* taking place.

The river of living spiritual water is *now* emerging from this church and individual temple to bless a needy world (Ezek. 47:1-12; Joel 3:18; Zech. 14:8; John 7:37-39; 4:10, 14; Rev. 22:17). The spiritual latter rain is *now* falling and is experienced by thousands of Christians in all parts of the world. Their experience harmonizes with the interpretation (Joel 2:23-29; Zech. 10:1). The spiritual gathering of God's people is *now* taking place (Rev. 18:4; Isa. 11:11, 12). From the confusion of Babylon they come to Jerusalem, "the foundations of peace." The walls of spiritual Jerusalem are *now* being built (Isa. 60:1-11). Each believer is conscious of the protecting Presence of God (Zech. 2:5). In the Person of His Holy Spirit, Jesus is *now* reigning in spiritual Jerusalem (Micah 4:7; Joel 3:17, 21; Isa. 24:23; Ezek. 48:35, etc.).

Those "in Christ" know this by joyful experience. Satan is *now* endeavoring to assemble his hosts against spiritual Israel (Ezek. 38, 39; Joel 3; Zech. 14). The sincere believer knows from his daily experience that he fights the good fight of faith against wicked spirits in high places. He fights best who, morning by morning, visualizes the battlefield and nerves himself for conflict with the combined forces under Gog's—Satan's—banner, and who marches into the field of battle "with the cross of Jesus going on before." The utter defeat of the enemies of God's people, so graphically depicted in Ezek. 38, 39, is the blessed assurance to His people that they are the recipients of His care and protection, and that they will triumph over their enemies.

"Now thanks be unto God, which always causeth us to triumph in Christ" (2 Cor. 2:14). Israel's victory depicted in Ezek. 38, 39; Joel 3; Zech. 14, has a *daily* significance to the Christian when (as it should be) it is applied in harmony with his experience; but these prophecies, when applied literally in relation to nations yet to war in Palestine can have no significance to the Christian's present experiences. When these prophecies are applied to the future of the nations of the world it may please the mind, but it can have no message to the heart of the Christian; it cannot be of spiritual help to the Christian in his fight against the forces of evil arrayed against him. But it should be remembered that God did not inspire men to write prophecies—especially long prophecies such as Ezek. 38, 39—merely to pass on matters of purely mental interest; He caused to be written that which would help Christians in their conflict with the forces of evil. Since the rejection of the

Jewish nation as God's chosen nation, the prophecies concerning Israel meet their fulfillment in relation to the church of God—the spiritual Israel (Gal. 6:16, etc.). Prophecies depicting a gathering of evil forces against "Israel" now describe the spiritual warfare. "They shall surely gather together, but not by Me: whosoever shall gather together against thee shall fall for thy sake. . . . No weapon that is formed against thee shall prosper" (Isa. 54:15, 17). In his *daily* experience the earnest Christian says: "Though an host should encamp against me, my heart shall not fear" (Ps. 27:3).

Chapter Eleven

APPLYING THE PRINCIPLE IN CONNECTION WITH THE STUDY OF "ARMAGEDDON"

Applying the principle of the harmony of interpretation and Christian experience in connection with the Revelator's description of Armageddon (Rev. 16:12-16), we learn that, as a description of a military battle between nations in Palestine, it has no message for the Christian in his conflict with the powers of evil. When interpreted as the finale of the great controversy between Christ and Satan, it immediately becomes of great interest and usefulness to the Christian who is *now* engaged in warfare with the forces of evil. The very first promise given was one in which the Lord promised man that He would be with him in the conflict with the forces of evil (see Gen. 3:15). In God's Word, throughout the centuries we can trace the development of that "war" or "controversy." We are admonished to "endure hardness, as a *good soldier of Jesus Christ*" (2 Tim. 2:3), and to "*war* a good *warfare*" (1 Tim. 1:18). By the word "war" or "battle" the Revelator describes the great controversy between Christ and Satan from the time they warred in heaven until the consummation of all things at the end of the millennium (see Rev. 12:7, 17; 13:7; 16:14, 16; 17:14; 19:19; 20:8). The purpose for which the Bible was written was to make the child of God wise regarding the spiritual "war," and to give him strength to "*fight* the good *fight of faith*" (1 Tim. 6:12). When the Lord's prophets describe the spiritual conflict which wages between those serving in the Lord's army and those on the side of the Lord's enemy, they liken the Christian to a soldier, with his armor on, fighting with a *spiritual* sword—the Word of God (see Ephes. 6:11-17). This conflict is as real as any war between nations, is more continuous and more extensive than any material struggle between nations, and requires from the Christian as much patience, perseverance, and ceaseless struggle as in any international conflict. The knowledge of this Bible teaching has prompted hymn writers to write such hymns as: "Onward. Christian soldiers! *Marching as to war.*" Under such names as "Armageddon," and "The Final Conflict," hymnologists have given the Christian church hymns which express the inspired interpretation of the "war" imagery of the Apocalypse. These godly hymn writers have expressed the interpretation held by the most spiritual and devoted men and women of God. The Christian church has lost its power for the battle against evil in proportion to its loss of the spiritual vision accorded by the true interpretation of these "war" pictures of the Revelation. Satan's design is to weaken the church by spreading abroad false interpretations, which cause people to fail to see their own personal and vital connection with the battle between the forces of good and evil: that they are either on the Lord's side in His army, or on the side of the Lord's enemy. By teaching that these prophecies deal with some material war among nations away off in Palestine, people are blinded to the solemn truth that these "war" pictures of the Revelation were given by our Lord to show that by our acceptance or rejection of Him and His truth, we either stand with Him or against Him.

If "Armageddon" concerned merely a future Palestinian military war, it could have no present or future spiritual value to the Christian, for it would belong *entirely* to the future; but as the conclusion of the spiritual conflict, it has a definite message for those *now* engaged in that warfare. If "the kings from the sunrising" refer to military powers who come into the prophetic limelight only at the time of the sixth plague, the prophecy could have no message for anyone *until the time of the sixth plague, and even at that time such information would help no one!* But when "the Kings from the sunrising" are interpreted as the heavenly armies led by our Lord Jesus Christ coming to deliver His people and to destroy their Babylonian enemies, the prophecy is immediately lifted to the plane of being a present blessing to believers in the Lord. A prophecy of future *military* events would be limited to the time referred to, and would mean just that, and no more, being totally independent of Christian experience; but, as the writer has shown in a larger publication, prophecies concerning future events in the great conflict between the forces of good and evil have a present blessing for those engaged in that conflict. The Leader of the forces of good, and the leader of the forces of evil, and the principles involved are the same down through all stages of the spiritual conflict, and, as shown in my previous publication referred to, a prophetic description of its final stages, in principle, is applicable to other parts of the conflict. After the 1,000 years mentioned in Rev. 20, the wicked seek to overthrow the saints; but they have sought to do that down through all the centuries of the conflict. The Lord reigning within the New Jerusalem thwarts the purpose of the wicked and destroys the enemies of His people; but the Lord has always reigned within the midst of His people and always caused them to triumph—even in the face of adversity.

Christian experience is in harmony with the interpretation that "the Kings from the sunrising" refers to the coming of the heavenly armies led by our Lord. Having fully explained all the angles of this prophecy in other publications, we must refer the reader to them for detailed consideration. Here, where we are necessarily restricted by space, we confine our remarks to that which particularly concerns Christian experience and Christ as "*the sunrising.*"

Throughout the Scriptures Christ is said to be the "Day-spring," or "*Sunrising*" (see Luke 1:78, margin; Mal. 4:2, etc.). He is declared to be "the Light of the world" (see John 9:5; 1:5, 9; 3:19; 8:12; 12:35, 46; Ephes. 5:14; 2 Pet. 1:19; Rev. 2:28; 22:16, etc.). These oft-repeated, explicit statements should guide Christ-loving Bible students when interpreting Rev. 16:12. In the Revelation (5:5) Jesus, the Son of David, is declared to be "the Lion of the tribe of Judah." As the tribe and standard of Judah were "on the east side toward the *rising of the sun*" (Num. 2:1-3), we know that the Revelator's reference to "the Lion of the tribe of Judah" keeps before us the connection of the east with Jesus, as "the Lion of the tribe of Judah" Who leads His people across the sands of the desert to the Promised Land. In the Scriptures the lion is employed as the symbol of strength to destroy one's enemies, and when Jesus comes the second time He is pictured as Israel's "strong Redeemer" (Jer. 50:34) coming from the east—"from the rising of the sun"—like Cyrus (whose name meant "the sun") to liberate Israel from the bondage of Babylon (Jer. 50:33; Isa. 41:2, 25; 45:1, 13; 46:11).

The same Greek word for "east" ("anatole") is employed in Rev. 7:2 (where a message from Christ is pictured as coming from the "east"), and Rev. 16:12. The same word, "anatole," is also employed in Luke 1:78, where Jesus is definitely termed "the Dayspring," or "*Sunrising.*" Zacharias declared, "The *Dayspring*" (margin, "*Sunrising*") from on high hath visited us, to give *light* to them that sit in *darkness* and in the shadow of death, to guide our feet into the way of peace."

Jesus is the Source of spiritual light, comfort and growth of the soul as the sun is the source of literal light, warmth and growth of all things on this world. Without the light of the sun all earthly life would perish; without the light of Jesus all spiritual life would perish. This truth is well expressed in the words of the hymn written by John Wesley, "Christ, Whose Glory," and in such hymns as "Sun of My Soul," "Jesus, the Light of the World," etc.

Christ is said to be "the light of men," "that light," "the true light" (John 1:4, 7, 8). John declares that "God is light" (1 John 1:5). James states that God is "the Father of lights" (James 1:17). The Psalmist says: "The Lord God is a sun" (Ps. 84:11). Isaiah assures us that "the Lord shall be thine everlasting light, and thy God thy glory" (Isa. 60:20, 21). "The Lord is my light" (Ps. 27:1). "The light dwelleth with Him" (Dan. 2:22). Jesus came to be "a light to lighten the Gentiles" (Luke 2:32). "Christ shall give thee light" (Ephes. 5:14). "Come, let us walk in the light of the Lord" (Isa. 2:5). "And in Thy light we shall see light" (Ps. 36:9). "The saints in light" (Col. 1:12). "The light of the gospel" (2 Cor. 4:4). "His marvelous light" (1 Pet. 2:9). The gospel church is likened to "a woman clothed with the sun" (Rev. 12:1). "The law is light" (Prov. 6:23). "Thy word is a lamp unto

my feet, and a light unto my path" (Ps. 119:105). "The entrance
of Thy words giveth light" (Ps. 119:130). "The path of the just
is as the shining light" (Prov. 4:18). These are a few of scores
of such expressions to be found throughout the Word of God.
Christ's kingdom is depicted in the Scriptures as the kingdom
of light (Luke 16:8, etc.), and Satan's kingdom as the kingdom
of darkness (Ephes. 6:12; Col. 1:13, etc.).

It should be emphasized that the light from Jesus, "the Light
of the world," "the Sun of righteousness," *comes to believers as the
sun rising in the eastern skies*, scattering the darkness and giving
light to those who previously were in darkness. "His *going forth*
is prepared *as the morning*" (Hos. 6:3). "Then shall thy light break
forth *as the morning*" (Isa. 58:8). "Until the *day dawn*, and the *day
star arise* in your hearts" (2 Pet. 1:19). "But unto you . . . shall the
Sun of righteousness *arise*" (Mal. 4:2). "I am . . . the bright and
morning star" (Rev. 22:16).

The blessings of the light of the gospel are spoken of as
coming from the east. "*Arise*, shine; for thy light is come, and
the glory of the Lord is *risen* upon thee. For, behold, the darkness
shall cover the earth, and gross darkness the people: but the Lord
shall *arise* upon thee, and His glory shall be seen upon thee. And
the Gentiles shall come to thy light, and kings to the brightness
of thy *rising*" (Isa. 60:1-3). Upon a world of spiritual darkness
the light of the gospel message is shining. Coming from "the Sun
of righteousness"; coming *like the rising of the sun* (Rev. 7:1-3),
its glory is now being shed with increasing power throughout the
earth. Soon "the earth" will be "lightened with His glory" (Rev.
18:1). Thus the Scriptures refer to the *spiritual light of the gospel
coming* "from the east" or "*from the sunrising*," and also refer to
the *literal* glory of Christ coming "from the east" or "*from the
sunrising*" (Matt. 24:27; Rev. 16:12, etc.).

*Christian experience harmonizes with the interpretation
that applies* (Rev. 16:12) *in connection with Christ and His
glorious work of redemption*. Light is actually a ray of power and
energy. Gospel light is a vibrant power poured out by "the Sun
of righteousness" upon those who seek for it. Light is energy-
giving and strengthens the innermost soul. It penetrates the soul

and the mind, and these react on the physical and will make it well and happy. Light from "the Sun of righteousness" descends upon honest hearts and uplifts, exalts, refines and purifies. Light is the giver of all things worthwhile. All evil flies before it like bats before the dawn. All things of menace to mankind thrive in the dark. All things of Light glory in the Light. Light glorifies the colors of the earth and uplifts humanity in its appreciation of the beautiful. Light is being used in its many forms in hospitals today to rejuvenate people and heal the sick. The gospel light is shining and is healing sin-sick souls. Rev. 16:12 teaches that the Light-giver is coming back with the hosts of light to destroy the kingdom of darkness. As the *rising of the sun* is a *daily* experience, so the believer in Jesus knows that the "healing" rays of "the Sun of righteousness" (Mal. 4:2) rise *daily* upon him, dispelling the darkness. *Every day his life harmonizes with the true interpretation of Rev. 16:12.* By interpreting Rev. 16:12-16 in relation to a future military war, the moral purpose of this prophecy is lost sight of and Satan is gratified.

The Revelator's reference to the drying up of the river Euphrates (Rev. 16:12) when applied militarily in regard to the future is meaningless to Christians living today; but when applied, as it should be, in connection with the conflict between the forces of good and evil, it has a spiritual message for each Christian today. Babylon was built upon the Euphrates, the waters of which were predicted to dry up (Jer. 50:38; 51:36; Isa. 44:27). This provides the Revelator with the expression which he uses in Rev. 16:12. John obtained his imagery regarding spiritual Babylon from Isaiah's forecasts of the destruction of literal Babylon by Cyrus, who is a type of Christ. The translators believed that the Revelator used the drying up of the river Euphrates in the taking of ancient Babylon to obtain his imagery for the overthrow of spiritual Babylon for, in the margin of Rev. 16:12, they have placed Jer. 50:38; 51:36, which prophesied the drying up of the river Euphrates. And that they regarded the reference to "the kings of the east" as referring back to the overthrow of ancient Babylon by Cyrus is evident by the fact that they placed Isa. 41:2, 25, which predicted the coming of one "from the east," "from the rising of the sun," in the margin of Rev. 16:12. In Isa. 44:24-28; 45:1, Cyrus is set forth as a type of the Messiah. Cyrus overthrowing the literal, ancient Babylon after the drying of the Euphrates, is a type of Christ overthrowing spiritual Babylon after drying up the flooding, persecuting waters of modern Babylon by the manifestations of His "fury" (Ezek. 38:18), which arrest the attempt of murderous Babylonian "multitudes" (Rev. 17:1, 15) to slay the people of God.

It is clear that the prophecies of Isaiah relating to the coming of the Almighty Saviour of Israel to bring in "everlasting salvation" and "the world without end" are linked up with Cyrus, the Lord's "Anointed" ("Messiah"), who destroyed literal Babylon (see Isaiah, chapters 41-48).

The name "Cyrus" means "the sun," and Cyrus in his work of destroying Babylon and delivering Israel, typifies Jesus "the Sun of righteousness" (Mal. 4:2). The references to Cyrus coming "from the east," "from the *rising of the sun*," are a play upon the meaning of his name. There is also a spiritual play upon the designation of Jesus as "the *Sun* of righteousness" Who *arises* "with healing in His wings." Jesus is the true "Sunrising": "The *Sunrising* from on high" came "to give *light* to them that sit in *darkness*" (Luke 1:78, 79 margin; Isa. 9:2; 42:6, 7). Obviously the things Isaiah wrote concerning Cyrus (Isa. 45:1, 3, 13; 46:11, etc.) typify the greater redemption to be wrought out by the greater Cyrus, the greater "Shepherd-King," God's "Anointed" or "Messiah," the Deliverer of spiritual Israel.

After having introduced Cyrus in Isa. 41, verses 1-7 of chapter 42, etc., outline the work of God's "servant"—the coming Messiah—Who would "bring out the prisoners from the prison, and them that sit in *darkness* out of the prison house" (Isa. 42:7). As Cyrus, the Lord's "anointed" (Isa. 45:1), set Israel free (Isa. 45:13), so the greater Cyrus, the Lord's "Anointed" (Isa. 61:1), would "proclaim *liberty* to the captives, and the *opening of the prison* to them that are bound" (Isa. 61:1). Thus the Messiah's work of redemption is described in connection with the prophecy concerning the work of Cyrus in liberating Israel from their Babylonian captivity. But one does not need to wait until the sixth plague for the Lord to intervene and dry up the waters of the Euphrates and bring deliverance to those in Babylonian captivity. Today our Lord will bring deliverance from the bondage of sin; today, He will set His people free (Luke 4:18-21) and dry up the waters that threaten to engulf them (see Isa. 43:2; 59:19; 8:7; 28:1,2; 2 Sam. 22:5; Ps. 69:1, 2, 14, 15).

To further illustrate the principle that a true interpretation of the prophecies—particularly those picturing earth's final events—will always be a "revelation of Jesus Christ" as the Saviour of His people, and the Destroyer of their enemies, and that it will also have a bearing upon present Christian experience, we will touch briefly upon the book of Daniel.

Chapter Twelve

THE MORAL PURPOSE OF THE PROPHECIES OF DANIEL

Prophecies were not written *merely* as milestones to the kingdom of God. While the church may find joy in measuring the distance still to travel on the highway of time, by noting how many milestones have been passed and how many more there are yet to pass before the coming of Christ, it should be emphasized that this is not their greatest purpose. The prophecy of Daniel, chapter two, was given to teach that the rise and fall of empires is not due to the fluctuating fortunes of monarchs and dictators, but to the overruling providence of God (Dan. 2:20-22); that nations are overthrown when they oppose and hinder God's moral purpose in the earth; that because men are selfish they cannot build a lasting empire; that God will establish a kingdom made up of people who have learned to obey the will of God. In Matt. 21:44 *Jesus applies this prophecy in connection with the individual* who either accepts or rejects the gospel. Our Lord does not employ this prophecy to declare that the fourth of the kingdoms (represented by the legs of iron) had come, therefore the end must be drawing near, but He did apply the setting up of the kingdom of stone—His own everlasting kingdom—in relation to the present and *applied it to the moral choice of the individual*.

Daniel, chapter three, shows the conflict between the kingdoms of God and of Satan. The king of Babylon, under Satan's leadership (see Isa. 14:4, 12), sought to frustrate the fulfillment of the prophecy given by Daniel recorded in the previous chapter. In his efforts he endeavoured to compel the Hebrews to break God's moral Law. The book of Revelation applies this moral conflict between the law of the king of Babylon and the Law of God in connection with the present and in connection with the individual. The people in literal Babylon were to "*worship* the golden *image*" that Nebuchadnezzar, the king of Babylon, had set up. This fact is stated six times—Dan. 3:5, 7, 10, 12, 14, 18. In the Revelation, God's warning against *worshipping* the beast and his "*image*" is mentioned six times—Rev. 13:15; 14:9, 11; 16:2; 19:20; 20:4. "If *any man* worship the beast and his image."

God's care over His loyal children is illustrated by the fact that He "*delivered* His servants that trusted in Him" (Dan. 3:28). Daniel, chapter six, reveals the plottings of men and demons to turn people from their allegiance to the Law of God, and the testing and the triumph through God's power of those who remain loyal to Him. Again, the emphasis is placed upon the *deliverance* of those who *serve* God "continually" (see Dan. 6:14, 16, 20-27). The deliverance mentioned in Dan. 12:1 is not unrelated to the other deliverances mentioned earlier in the book of Daniel; but, rather, the previous deliverances illustrate the deliverance mentioned in Dan. 12:1. The purpose for which the last, long prophecy of Daniel was written was not to point to a supposed gathering of nations to Palestine for an "Armageddon" which has nothing to do with God's moral purpose (a war between nations has no moral significance for the Christian's own experience). Actually this prophecy says absolutely nothing regarding a supposed conflict of nations in Palestine; it says nothing concerning a military "Armageddon," but it does point to *the deliverance from death at the hands of spiritual Babylon of those who have obeyed the Law of God.*

The time of trouble mentioned in Dan. 12:1 occurs at the time of the outpouring of the seven last plagues of Rev. 16. When Jesus ("Michael") stands up He ceases to mediate on man's behalf; no longer will His intercession hold back the winds of strife and worldwide commotion and trouble. Today Jesus intercedes on behalf of those who are seeking Divine aid in the development of character. This prophecy warns of the time when Jesus' intercessory work will cease. It is to this great decisive event that Dan. 12:1 points us. The eternal destiny of all the human family will then have been decided. Surely this is a most solemn moral reason for giving this prophecy. When Jesus completes His heavenly ministry the seven last plagues of Rev. 16 fall upon those who have rejected Christ's last-day Message; they fall upon people *because they have worshipped* the beast and his image (Rev. 16:2), and because they have planned the death of God's people (v. 5, 6, etc.). They fall upon "the seat of the beast and his kingdom" (v. 10); they fall upon "*Babylon*" (v. 19). To interpret the sixth plague in connection with purely military matters is distinctly out of harmony with God's clearly-stated moral purpose for sending the plagues. The plagues are poured upon the devotees of a false system of worship; upon those who worship the beast and his image; upon those who, by following that false system of worship, are found living in disobedience to the Holy Law of God. The plagues are definitely said to be *Babylon's* plagues (see Rev. 16:19; 18:4, 8, 10, etc.).

In the first chapter of Daniel we see demonstrated the fact that eating good food is important in the life of the Christian. Clean, wholesome foods affect clean living and clear thinking. The Christian needs all the mental and spiritual strength he can muster in the great battle of life. In Daniel, chapter one, God shows the moral connection between food and religion; He indicates that the deep prophecies of Daniel will be better understood when care is observed in eating the best available foods.

In the other chapters of Daniel (which in this brief outline we have not directly discussed), their moral purpose is surely patent to all who have adequately studied them. In chapter four, pride is humbled. Chapter five teaches nations and individuals that there is a limit to sin and blasphemy beyond which they are not permitted to pass. The close of spiritual Babylon's probation to which we are directed in Dan. 12:1, is illustrated by the close of literal Babylon's probation mentioned in Daniel, chapter 5. The downfall of literal Babylon by armies from the east (Isa. 41:2; 46:11) occurred after their probation had closed (Dan. 5:27-30), just as the downfall of spiritual Babylon by armies from heaven appearing in the eastern skies (Rev. 16:12; 19:11-20) will occur after their probation has closed (Rev. 15:6-8; 18:4-8).

In the seventh chapter of Daniel we trace the onward course of the controversy between Christ and Satan from literal Babylon, the center of Satan's kingdom, down to spiritual Babylon, which is now the center of Satan's kingdom. Satan's kingdom succeeds in persuading people that the Law of God has been changed (Dan. 7:25), but the Judgment sits (Dan. 7:9-13) and Christ's kingdom will be eventually established and peopled by those who remain loyal to the moral law (Dan. 7:14, 22, 26, 27).

In chapters eight and nine the moral purpose of prophecy is conspicuously manifest. The emphasis is upon God's true system of worship and Satan's counterfeit system of worship. Verses 23-25 of chapter eight depict the work of both pagan and papal Rome; pagan Rome's depredations were against the literal Jews; papal Rome's depredations were against the spiritual Jews. Once again papal Rome, which is the center of Satan's kingdom—spiritual Babylon of the book of Revelation—is connected up with ancient Babylon. The 2,300 days of Dan. 8:14, and the 70 weeks (of this time period) which were cut off upon the literal nation of Israel (Dan. 9:24) were to commence with the decree enabling the Jews to return to Palestine from their Babylonian captivity. The Babylonians had destroyed their temple and their beloved city, Jerusalem (2 Chron. 36:19; Dan. 9:16-19), and the providences of God enabled them to go out of Babylon and return to rebuild and restore the temple and Jerusalem and their national life (Dan. 9:25). Subtracting the 70 weeks or 490 years, allotted to the Jews as their probationary period, from the 2,300 days or years, leaves 1810 years. Many expositors have seen that this long prophecy terminates in or about 1844. But how do they apply this prophecy and in what connection? They apply it in connection with the return of the *literal* Jews to Palestine, and their eventual *national* rehabilitation. In this way they lose sight of the *moral* purpose of prophecy in connection with the present spiritual kingdom of our Lord. The coming out of Babylon by the ancient people of God is applied in Rev. 18:4 in connection with *the moral choice of* people who heed the call of Christ to serve Him and to leave spiritual Babylon, the place of false worship. In the New Testament, the "temple" is applied in connection with the moral condition of a group of people (the church) or of each individual. Thus the *national* application of events to transpire at the terminal of the 2,300 days' prophecy forsakes the moral application employed in the New Testament. Today, God's people are coming out of spiritual Babylon and are returning to spiritual Jerusalem, and are repairing the breaches in the wall of the city of our God, and the temple service of true worship is being rebuilt.

Chapter Thirteen

CHRISTIAN REALITIES REVEALED IN THE PROPHETIC PICTURES OF THE APOCALYPSE

The Christian life is very real, and God desires to help His children grasp its realities. Rightly understood, the Apocalypse provides *prophetic pictures* which enable the Christian to *visualize* the actualities of the spiritual conflict. One writer has stated: "Could our spiritual vision be quickened, we should see souls bowed under oppression and burdened with grief. . . . We should see angels flying quickly to the aid of these tempted ones, forcing back the hosts of evil that encompass them, and placing their feet on a firm foundation. *The battles waging between the two armies are as real as those fought by the armies of this world*, and on the issue of the *spiritual conflict* eternal destinies depend" (*Prophets and Kings*, p. 176).

The more the Christian remembers that this conflict is constantly being waged, the more he realizes what is transpiring around him and in connection with his own salvation, the more alert, watchful and prepared will he be. Satan ever seeks to make the realities appear unreal or far-removed. The unseen and eternal become vague and shadowy. The urgency and the necessity for watchfulness are dulled by a multitude of worldly things—things which seem so very real, but after all are not the real things. Paul declared: "While we look not at the things which are seen, but at the things which are not seen: for the things which are seen are temporal; but *the things which are not seen are eternal*" (2 Cor. 4:18).

Christians have to fight against the ever-present tendency to relegate spiritual realities to the background and to permit the temporal things of this world to hide the eternal, unseen things.

To help the Christian fasten clear pictures upon his mind and to draw from them strength and comfort, God caused the prophets to employ arresting, colorful imagery in their prophetic descriptions. Educationalists rightly stress the value of "visual education." Because God has endowed the mind with the ability to make *pictures*—to *visualize* what we read or hear—He has so inspired the writing of His Holy Word that it forms a long gallery of *word pictures*—"likenesses," "similitudes," "imagery."

The historical incidents recorded in the Old Testament provide us with *word pictures* by which God teaches us spiritual truths. In them we are to see things worldwide in scope: *corresponding likenesses in the spiritual realm*, which are "spiritually discerned" (1 Cor. 2:14). The New Testament, and particularly the Revelation, reveals the principle of *"spiritually"* discerning "spiritual things" in the historical narratives of the Old Testament. The natural eye does not see these "spiritual things," and often interprets literally that which should be *"spiritually* discerned" (see 1 Cor. 2:6-16).

In the Old Testament, seven golden candlesticks provided the only light in the Jewish sanctuary; in the first chapter of Revelation those seven candlesticks *represent* the experience of the Christian church throughout the Christian era (Rev. 1:20). Like its divine Author, the church is "the light of the world" (Matt. 5:14; John 9:5). The *picture* provided of a world in darkness only lit by the church should act as a stimulant to provoke zeal in letting the light of the Saviour shine forth in all its splendor. In a previous publication, the writer has shown that the Revelation, throughout, employs the principle that the things of the Old Testament provide *imagery* in depicting worldwide things in connection with our Lord and His church—and their enemies.

The Revelation is rich in *word pictures*, and sometimes errors are conceived and advocated by those who interpret *literally* all the details of these graphic descriptions, instead of *symbolically* as they should be interpreted. We cite but a few examples.

The doctrines of eternal torment and a red devil with a tail, etc., have their basis in taking with rigid literality figures of speech and symbols (see Rev. 12:3, 4; Isa. 14:9-20; Ezek. 32:18-32; Luke 16:19-31, etc.).

The emblems of our Lord's broken body and His shed blood—the bread and the wine used in the Lord's Supper—are *spiritual symbols*. By taking *literally* Christ's statement: "This is My body . . . this is My blood," Roman Catholics have been led into the error of transubstantiation. Protestants repudiate the idolatry of the Mass by interpreting Christ's statement *symbolically*, and *not* literally. Error is often the *literal* interpretation of *that which God intended to be applied spiritually*.

The four celestial beings of Rev. 7:1-3 are not *literally* stationed in the four quarters of the earth, for the purpose of checking and restraining *literal* winds that blow from the four points of the compass. It is a *symbolical* representation of the Lord's control, through His angelic ministers, of world affairs so that they do not prevent the completion of His work on earth.

"Ascending from the east" (v. 2): a message comes from Christ as the sun comes forth *with increasing splendor* until the meridian glory is reached (see Rev. 18:1). Thus light is to increase until the end. The prophetic picture concerning the coming of the angel from the east, four angels holding the four winds, and the sealing of the tribes of Israel, is *not* to be taken *literally*, but as a *symbolical* representation of the completion of the work of Christ on earth. A well-known writer has stated:—

> "'The four corners of the earth,' and the 'four winds of the earth, are evidently phrases which are meant to convey the idea of the worldwide extent of the conditions which the Revelator is describing. The seal of the living God, and the white robes, and the twelve tribes are also symbols, for no one would suppose that a literal seal was to be actually stamped upon the foreheads of God's servants; nor that the saints literally washed their robes in the blood of Christ, nor that the sealing work was confined to the twelve literal tribes of Israel, of whom all means of identification have been lost for many centuries. . . . *Much of the real meaning of such passages of Scripture as Rev. 7 is lost when an attempt is made to deal with them literally. Beautiful truths are revealed in these symbolic passages*, once we can define the symbolism which is used" (*The World's Finale*, pp. 69-72, by A. W. Anderson, emphasis mine).

In order to enable His children to grasp the grandeur of spiritual truths that will strengthen and encourage, that will arrest attention and powerfully impress, God inspired His prophets to paint prophetic pictures that will make what He seeks to impart *stand out as though literally happening before our eyes*. It would help readers of the Apocalypse to obtain a correct understanding of the moral purpose of the Apocalypse if it were remembered that the church is pictured as *if it were* Israel dwelling in Canaan and re-living the experiences of ancient Israel. As the Christian life is powerfully illustrated by the *typical* experiences of literal Israel (1 Cor. 10:1-11, margin, etc.), so experiences befalling the Christian church and described in the prophecies of the Apocalypse are also depicted *as if the church as Israel still dwells in the Holy Land*. Many commentators have drawn attention to this fact. A *Commentary on the New Testament*, published by the "Society for Promoting Christian Knowledge," says on its notes dealing with the battle of Armageddon: "We must remember that throughout this Book *Canaan represents the locality of the church of God*. The quarter from which enemies gathered against the earthly Canaan was the North. Then from the banks of the Euphrates came the Assyrian . . . the Chaldean, the destroyer of Jerusalem. . . . We are not to think here of any great battle to be fought on this actual spot [Megiddo]. This were to forget what is ever to be borne in mind, that throughout this Book, Jerusalem, Sion, the Holy Land and various localities in it are *symbols* of the Christian church, its sanctuary, or its enemies. . . . The battle is a *figure*, as naturally employed, as the words by which we describe the prevalence of good over evil, in which it is almost impossible not to use expressions borrowed from the battlefield—struggle, defeat, triumph, victory, and the like. The Visions of the Apocalypse are to the eye what metaphorical words are to the ears—*symbols*, ideal, not real, pictures of what is to come to pass."

Anciently Israel was referred to as "a people *near* unto Him" (Ps. 148:14). The sanctuary and, later, the temple, the dwelling place of God, was located in the midst of Israel. Israel encamped about and near to the sanctuary, while the gentile world was far-removed; a people "afar off." This *physical* fact is employed by Paul to *picture* a spiritual truth. Writing of believers now being the Israel of God and those not "in Christ" as the "Gentiles," Paul says to those who had previously been classified as "Gentiles": "Wherefore remember, that ye being in time past Gentiles in the flesh. . . . That at that time ye were without Christ, being aliens from *the commonwealth of Israel*. But now in Christ Jesus ye who sometime *were far off are made nigh* by the blood of Christ. . . . And came and preached peace to you which *were afar off*, and to them that were nigh" (Ephes. 2:11-22). Thus Paul pictures the church now made up of Jews and Gentiles *as if it were* Israel living *"near"* to God in Jerusalem, while unbelievers are pictured as "Gentiles" "afar off." Jesus, the Revelator (see Rev. 22:16), represents the church *as if it were "with* Him" "on the mount Sion" (Rev. 14:1). In Rev. 11:1, 2 the church is pictured *as if it were* "the temple" and "the holy city." In Rev. 14:20 the destruction of the wicked is *symbolized* as grapes being trodden in a winepress "without the city." The city, of course (until after the 1,000 years), referring here to the church of God. The 1,600 furlongs or 200 miles refers to the circuit of the Holy Oblation where, in his *symbolic* vision of the church, Ezekiel pictures a mighty temple and city on the "very high mountain" "in the land of Israel." John applies this vision concerning the city, temple and Holy Oblation in "the land of Israel" in a worldwide sense.

In his *Notes on the Book of Revelation*, the Rev. A. Barnes says on the phrase "And the winepress was trodden without the city": "The *representation* was made *as if it were* outside of the city; that is, the city of Jerusalem, for that is *represented* as the abode of the holy. . . . The winepress was usually in the vineyard—not in a city—and this is the representation here. As appearing to the eye of John, it was not within the walls of any city, but standing without. And blood came out of the winepress. The *representation* is, that there would be a great destruction which would be well *represented* by the juice flowing from a winepress. Even unto the horse-bridles. Deep—as blood would be in a field of slaughter where it would come up to the very bridles of the horses. The idea is, that there would be a great slaughter. . . . The enemies of the church would be completely and finally overthrown, and that the church, therefore, delivered from all its enemies, would be triumphant."

These graphic portrayals were designed to cheer the hearts of the faithful and to console them in their trials and persecutions. Satan, seeking to divert the eyes of saints from the assurance these verses contain for them that their foes would be overthrown, causes erroneous ideas to be promulgated that these verses have reference to a literal, military conflict in Palestine outside of the city of Jerusalem; that the 200 miles refers to the length of Palestine, etc.

As the enemies of God and of His church are *not literal* bunches of grapes (see Rev. 14:17-20), their *gathering* is *not a literal gathering*. God commands the angels: "*Gather* the clusters of the vine of the earth [i.e., the worldwide vineyard] . . . and the angel thrust in his sickle into the earth, and gathered the vine *of the earth*, and cast it into the *great* winepress of the wrath of God. And the winepress was trodden *without the city*." Those who are slaughtered in the destruction of Armageddon are said to perish "without the city"—the spiritual Zion, the spiritual Jerusalem. "For *in* mount Zion and *in* Jerusalem shall be deliverance" (Joel 2:32). Thus "deliverance" is assured those who, heeding the call of Christ, "come out" of spiritual Babylon and enter into the spiritual city of Jerusalem.

The church is represented as being on Mount Zion "*with*" the Lord Jesus (Rev. 14:1). By a spiritual union they are just as much "*with Him*" (Rev. 17:14) *as if* they were there literally. When the kings of the earth—the governments of earth—"make war with the Lamb" His church is said to be "with Him" (see Rev. 17:12-14; 16:14-16; 19:19, 20). Thus the *gathering* of the nations to "make *war* against the Lamb" and His church is not a literal gathering to Mount Zion in the literal city of Jerusalem, but a *uniting* of the elements of Satan's kingdom into concerted action against the Lord's church, just *as if* there were two armies involved: one in Jerusalem, and the other gathered outside in "the valley of Jehoshaphat"—the valley of "God's Judgment." The gathering of the ripened grapes for the winepress outside the city of Jerusalem and Mount Zion and the gathering of *all* nations and people to fight against Christ and His church are both *symbolic representations* of the same events. The world's harvest which is mentioned in Rev. 14:14-20 is *pictured* as growing in "the valley of Jehoshaphat." Compare Joel 3:13 with Matt. 13:38-40, also Joel 3:13 with Rev. 14:14-20. By comparing Joel 3:2, 11, 12, with Matt. 25:31-33, we see that Jesus applies "the valley of Jehoshaphat" and the gathering of all the nations into it, as the *symbol* of the worldwide judgment of "all nations" at the time of His Second Advent. The *literal* application of these verses as a gathering of nations to war against each other hides the grandeur and the solemnity of the *symbolic* imagery portraying a moving, impressive picture representing the great Judgment day when all people—the sheep and the goats—will be judged and eternally separated.

Attempts to apply literally dramatic *symbolical* representations spoil the picture the inspired word-artist has painted and create absurdities, which not only hide the truth portrayed by the symbol, but which at times lead to superstition and error. As an example we cite Rev. 17:14—"These shall *make war with the Lamb*, and the Lamb shall overcome them." One earnestly writing in defense of the teaching that Armageddon pertains to nations in Palestine, after quoting Rev. 17:14, says: "Now it seems that when Jesus comes as King of kings and Lord of lords, the ten kingdoms will be in a position to oppose His cause." Another verse which is quoted in support of the belief that the nations are gathered by Satan to Palestine, and that at the second coming of Christ these nations make war against the Lord, is Rev. 19:19: "I saw the beast, and the kings of the earth, and their armies, *gathered together to make war against Him* that sat on the horse, and against His army."

What consummate folly to imagine an earthly army *literally* attacking the Almighty Son of God and the hosts of heaven at the Second Advent! The Second Advent will be the occasion of a greater display of Omnipotent power than is humanly conceivable. The brightness of Christ's coming destroys the wicked (2 Thess. 2:8, etc.). When the heavens open, as stated in Rev. 19:11, instead of the beast and the armies of earth (Rev. 19:19, 20) *literally* making war against the King of kings and His heavenly army, they flee in terror from the glory of the Lord, calling upon the mountains to hide them "from the face of Him that sitteth on the throne, and from the wrath of the Lamb" (see Rev. 6:14-17). It will be noted that in these verses the Revelator, as in Rev. 19:11-19, describes the *same* great day of the Lord, the *same* opening of the heavens, the *same* "kings of the earth, and the great men, and the rich men, and the chief captains, and the mighty men, and *every* bondman, and *every* free man*.*" Therefore it is obvious that the gathering together of "the beast, and the kings of the earth, and their armies" "to make war against Him that sat on the horse, and against His army" cannot possibly refer to a *literal* gathering of nations to Megiddo to *literally* fight against the Lord at His Second Advent, for "*all* men"—"*every* bondman and *every* free man"—will not be *literally* at Megiddo. Understood *symbolically*, we see that the unsaved of the whole world are *represented as if* they all served as divisions under the banner of Satan. The Revelator distinctly states that in this great army which he *symbolically* describes as being "gathered together" are "*all*" men, both free and bond, both small and great" (Rev. 19:17, 18). When the Lord, at His Second Advent, destroys "*all*" the unregenerate, though *symbolically* portrayed as armies gathered together and slain together, yet *literally* they are slain *by the Lord in all the world*. "*The slain of the Lord* shall be at that day *from one end of the earth even unto the other end of the earth*" (Jer. 25:33). Thus the gathering together of "*all* the fowls that fly" to eat the flesh of "*all* men" (Rev. 19:17, 18) could not be a *literal* gathering together of the birds to the literal land of Israel, for "*all* men" will be destroyed *by the Lord* "from one end of the earth even unto the other end of the earth." John obtains this imagery of the ignominy and the completeness of the destruction of the enemies of God from the prophecy concerning Gog and his army (see Ezek. 39:4, 17-20). This shows that Ezekiel's prophecy (chaps. 38, 39) must be understood as a *symbolical* presentation of the worldwide spiritual conflict, which ends in the final destruction of those who serve under the banner of Satan. In Rev. 20:8, 9, we have the Lord's interpretation of the prophecy of Ezekiel concerning the multitudes in the army of Gog—they are the multitudes deceived by Satan: the enemies of our Lord.

In Ps. 45:3-7 the Lord's *spiritual* conflict is presented *symbolically.* In Heb. 1:8, 9 these verses are applied to our Lord. The same *symbolic* description is employed in Rev. 19:11-14 to depict the Lord's return to complete His *warfare* against evil by destroying those who just previously endeavoured to persecute and destroy the people of God. The Revelator's description of Jesus coming with "the *armies*" of heaven to make "*war*" against the beast and the armies of earth is obviously intended to be understood *symbolically*. Will Jesus *literally* ride "a white horse" down the skies (Rev. 19:11)? The Revelator had previously pictured Him at His Second Advent *sitting on a cloud, with a sickle in His hand* (see Rev. 14:14-16). Will all the multiplied millions of angels *literally* "ride upon white horses" (Rev. 19:14)? Will a *literal* "sharp sword" come "out of His mouth" (vs. 15)? Our Lord's "sharp sword" is His word (see Heb. 4:12; Ephes. 6:17, etc.). Will He come *literally* "clothed with a vesture dipped in blood"? Will He then *literally* tread "the winepress" (Rev. 19:13, 15)? Will an angel *literally* invite "all the fowls that fly" to come "unto the supper of the great God" and "eat the flesh of kings, and the flesh of captains, and the flesh of mighty men, and the flesh of horses, and of them that sit on them, and the flesh of all men" (Rev. 19:17, 18)? "The beast, and the kings of the earth, and their armies" will not be *literally* "gathered together to make war against Him that sat on the horse, and against His army" (Rev. 19:19). Our Lord Jesus, the Revelator (Rev. 22:16), *symbolically* portrays the worldwide spiritual conflict. Any attempt to *literalize* this symbolic presentation *hides the moral purpose* which it was designed to portray.

A widely-read Christian writer, stressing the necessity of observing the *symbolic* character of the Apocalypse, says:—

"This book [Revelation] demands close, prayerful study, lest it be interpreted according to the ideas of men, and false construction be given to the sacred word of the Lord, which in *its symbols and figures* means so much to us. . . . *In the Revelation the deep things of God are portrayed*" (Ellen G. White, *Manuscript Releases,* vol 18, p 23, Ltr 16, 1900).

In accordance with the principle enunciated, this same author has often *symbolically* applied, in connection with the great controversy between Christ and Satan, the same passages of Scripture which we have been considering. Graphically depicting the conflict between the forces of good and evil, in harmony with what we have shown is the correct interpretation of the symbolic "war" passages presented in the Apocalypse, this popular author says:—

"I saw *two armies in terrible conflict.* One army was led by banners bearing the world's insignia; the other was led by the blood-stained banner of Prince Emmanuel. . . . Company after company from *the Lord's army* joined the foe, and tribe after tribe from the *ranks of the enemy* united with the commandment-keeping people of God. . . . The *battle* raged. Victory alternated from side to side. . . . The *Captain of our salvation* was ordering the *battle*, and sending support to His *soldiers.* His power was mightily displayed. . . . He led them on step by step, *conquering and to conquer.*

"At last the *victory* was gained. The *army* following the banner with the inscription, 'The commandments of God, and the faith of Jesus' (Rev. 14:12), was gloriously triumphant. . . . Now *the church is militant.* . . . But the day is coming in which the *battle* will have been fought, the victory won. . . . But the church must and will *fight* against seen and unseen foes. . . . Men have confederated *to oppose the Lord of hosts.* These confederacies will continue until Christ shall . . . put on the garments of vengeance" (*Testimonies for the Church*, vol. 8, pp. 41, 42).

Those who "come out" of Babylon (Rev. 18:4) and are gathered to be "*with*" Christ "on the mount Zion" have "the seal of God in their foreheads" (see Rev. 7:1-4; 14:1). Those who are gathered together to "*make war* with the Lamb" and they that are *with* Him (Rev. 17:14; 19:19) have "the mark of the beast" in their foreheads or in their hands (see Rev. 13:16, 17; 14: 9-11; 19:20). So vital it is for those living in this great hour of destiny to clearly understand the issues at stake, so important are the truths the Lord presents in the Apocalypse, that He throws living, symbolic pictures on the screen of prophecy to arrest and grip the attention. By interpreting these pictures *literally* in reference to Palestine (they are given in a Palestinian setting, for the church is *represented as if it were* with Christ on mount Zion, etc.), Satan causes Christ's important Apocalyptic messages to lose their meaning and their vitality.

Chapter Fourteen

"CHRIST IN YOU" — THE ASSURANCE OF VICTORY

There is no more necessary and no more comforting truth taught in Scripture than that our Lord Jesus Christ reigns in the heart of every believer. The frequency with which this sublime fact is stated in the New Testament should surely impress us with its great importance. The apostle Paul, whose extensive knowledge of the Old Testament and whose special tuition under the divine Teacher (see Gal. 1:12; Ephes. 3:3, etc.) gave him a crystal-clear interpretation of the prophecies concerning the Lord reigning in the midst of His people "Israel," triumphantly taught that the Lord Jesus reigns in the heart of each believer, as well as in the body of the church. He stated that he was especially endowed with wisdom "fully to preach the Word of God; even the mystery which hath been hid from ages and from generations, but *now is made manifest to His saints*: to whom God would make known what is the riches of the glory of this mystery *among the Gentiles*; which is *Christ in you*, the hope of glory" (Col. 1:25-27, margin).

The prophecies of the Old Testament declare that God—"the Holy One of Israel"—reigns "*in* Zion," and that by His Presence and power the enemies of Israel will be defeated and Israel triumph gloriously over them. (see Ps. 2:1-9; Joel 2:1, 15, 32; 3:16, 17, 21; Obad. 17; Micah 4:2, 7; Ezek. 39:7, etc.). Isaiah declared: "When the enemy shall come in like a flood, the Spirit of the Lord shall put him to flight [margin]. And *the Redeemer shall come to Zion*, and unto them that turn from transgression in Jacob, saith the Lord" (Isa. 59:19, 20). Notice Paul's inspired application of this verse in connection with the "Gentiles"—"aliens from the commonwealth of Israel" (Ephes. 2:12)—who, by their acceptance of Christ as Lord, then become members of "the Israel of God" (Gal. 6:16), being "no more strangers and foreigners, but fellow-citizens with the saints, and of the household of God" (Ephes. 2:19). Paul taught that the true Israel of God will be made up of sin-freed Jews and Gentiles: "And *so all Israel shall be saved: as it is written, There shall come out of Sion the Deliverer*, and shall *turn away ungodliness from Jacob*: For this is My covenant unto them, when *I shall take away their sin*" (Rom. 11:26, 27). Under the provisions of the New Covenant, God has promised to "subdue our iniquities" (Micah 7:19), to "take away our bent to sinning." Because God will not force the will, we must cooperate with Him by yielding our hearts to Him in a daily surrender. Thus, day-by-day, the Lord writes His Holy Law upon our hearts, as He has so graciously promised to do (Jer. 31:31-34; Heb. 8:8-12). We learn to say with the Psalmist: "O how love I thy Law! it is my meditation all the day" (Ps. 119:97). "Give us this day our *daily* bread" (Matt 6:11). "And He [Jesus] said to them all, If any man will come after Me, let him deny himself, and take up his cross *daily*, and follow Me" (Luke 9:23). "I die *daily*" (1 Cor. 15:31). "*Always* bearing about in the body the dying of the Lord Jesus, *that the life also of Jesus might be made manifest in our body. . . .* Yet the inward man is renewed *day by day*" (2 Cor. 4:10, 16).

The greatest problem in the world is, and has been since the inception of sin, that of personal, daily victory over sin. A hymn-writer has expressed man's great need:

> "And none, O Lord, have perfect rest,
> For none are wholly free from sin;
> And they who fain would serve Thee best,
> Are conscious most of wrong within."
>
> (A Methodist hymn, unknown author)

Christianity is more than the good news that God forgives sin; it also proclaims that God promises power, daily, to overcome sin. Another hymn-writer has expressed the desire of the sincere heart for this "double" or "perfect cure": "Be of sin the double cure, Save me from its *guilt* and *power*" (hymn, "Rock of Ages," Thomas Hastings).

Sin can be overcome only by Christ dwelling in the heart. This is the grand theme upon which the Apostle Paul frequently dwells. In his "much more" chapter (Romans 5) he declares with glowing eloquence: "*Much more*, then, being now justified by His blood, we shall be saved from wrath through Him. For if, when we were enemies, we were reconciled to God by the death of His Son, *much more*, being reconciled, *we shall be saved by His life. . . . Much more* they which receive abundance of grace and the gift of righteousness shall *reign in life by One*, Jesus Christ. . . . But where sin abounded, grace did much more abound: that as sin hath reigned unto death, even so might *grace reign* through righteousness unto eternal life by Jesus Christ our Lord" (Rom. 5:9-21). Sin brought man to a state of bondage from which he can never extricate himself. Being born with a sinful nature it is impossible for man to cease from sinning (Jer. 13:23; 17:9, etc.). But a life free from sin is assured all those who permit Jesus to reign upon the throne of the heart. Sin, as a powerful tyrant, reigns upon the heart and will drag man down to eternal destruction, but Jesus will save from sin all those who put their trust in Him. Sin is powerful, but "much more" strength is given the believer to "*reign in life* by one, Jesus Christ." "*Much more*, being reconciled, *we shall be saved by His life" lived out in the heart*. With Christ living and reigning upon the heart, victory over sin is assured.

In chapter six of Romans, Paul continues to emphasize this essential teaching of freedom from sin through the indwelling Christ. Instead of sin reigning in the heart (Rom. 6:12), the believer has Christ reigning in the heart and giving him freedom from the power of sin (see vs. 11, 12-22). After describing the battle against evil and the sincere soul's quest for holiness (Rom. 7), Paul then presents the secret of sanctification—*the indwelling Spirit of Christ*. He says: "For the law of the *Spirit of life* in Christ Jesus *hath made me free* from the law of sin and death. . . . If so be that the *Spirit of God dwell in you*. . . . And if *Christ be in you*. . . the Spirit is *life* because of righteousness. But if the *Spirit* of Him that raised up Jesus from the dead *dwell in you*, He that raised up Christ from the dead shall also *quicken* your mortal bodies by *His Spirit that dwelleth in you*" (Rom. 8:2-11). Victory over sin is assured through the indwelling, living, pulsating power of the Spirit of Christ, Who enlivens the mortal body and gives power to resist evil. Having shown that believing Jews and Gentiles alike partake of these privileges, Paul then applies, *in connection with a Christian's victory over sin*, Isaiah's prophecy of the coming of the Redeemer to Zion, the turning "from transgression in Jacob," and the putting of the enemy to flight.

Old Testament prophecies concerning the Lord reigning in Zion, and the victory of His people, are not to be understood as being separate from the story of salvation from sin, for salvation from sin *is* the moral purpose for which they were written. This interpretation of Old Testament prophecies was no doubt understood by some devout Israelites in ancient times, but from the day of Pentecost the Holy Spirit made this abundantly clear. Paul, in particular, was given special revelations to make these things clear to the Gentiles and to the "saints: to whom God would make known what is the riches of *the glory of this mystery* among the Gentiles; which is *Christ in you*, the hope of glory" (Col. 1:25-27).

In his "*Greek Dictionary of the New Testament*," Dr. Strong says concerning "Sion": "Figuratively, the *Church* (militant or triumphant)." Significant derivatives of the Hebrew for "Zion" are given as: "to glitter from afar, i.e., to be eminent; also to be permanent . . . strength, victory." Each believer in Christ may know from personal experience the present glorious fulfillment of Old Testament prophecies concerning the Lord reigning "*in* Zion," for from the Lord Jesus reigning upon the heart will come "strength" to live a life of "victory."

Victory over sin through the power of an indwelling Christ is "the hope of glory." "The *Spirit* of truth. . . He *dwelleth* with you, and shall be *in you*. . . . And *I in you*. . . . And *My Father* will love him, and *We* will come unto him, and make *Our abode with him*" (John 14:17-23). "What? know ye not that your body is the temple of the *Holy Ghost* which is *in you?*" (1 Cor. 6:19). *"God is in you"* (1 Cor. 14:25). *"Jesus Christ is in you"* (2 Cor. 13:5). "Ye are of God . . . and have overcome them: *because* greater is He that is *in you*, than he that is in the world" (1 John 4:4). "Strengthened with might by His Spirit *in the inner* man; that *Christ may dwell in your hearts by faith*" (Ephes. 3:16, 17). "I am crucified with Christ: nevertheless I live; yet not I, but *Christ liveth in me*: and the life which I now live in the flesh I live by the faith of the Son of God" (Gal. 2: 20).

In the words of the hymn "Live Out Thy Life Within Me," Frances R. Havergal has beautifully expressed the secret of personal victory over sin:

> "Live out Thy life within me,
> O Jesus King of kings!
> Be Thou Thyself the answer
> To all my questionings;
> Live out Thy life within me,
> in all things have Thy way!
> I, the transparent medium
> Thy glory to display.

> "The temple has been yielded,
> And purified of sin;
> Let Thy Shekinah glory
> Now shine forth from within."

In another hymn she wrote:

> "Take my heart, it is Thine own;
> It shall be *Thy royal throne*."

In Heb. 12:22 we read: "But ye *are come* unto mount Sion, and unto the city of the living God, the heavenly Jerusalem, and to an innumerable company of angels, to the general assembly and church of the firstborn." Sion is a heavenly mountain whose very name signifies sunny, and is the city of the living God. The expressions "mount Sion" and "the heavenly Jerusalem" not only refer to the future glorious capital of the Messiah's eternal kingdom in the earth made new (Rev. 21 and 22), but they refer to the *present* dwelling-place and throne of the Lord Jesus in His church and in each believer. Those who accept Jesus as their Lord and Saviour enter "the heavenly Jerusalem," and so long as they are loyal to the Commandments of God (Rev. 22:14) they are safe and secure *as if in a mighty fortress*. This expressive imagery is often presented in the Scriptures. Isaiah says: "In that day shall this song be sung in the land of Judah; *We have a strong city*; salvation will God appoint for walls and bulwarks. Open ye the gates, that the righteous nation which keepeth the truth may enter in. Thou wilt keep him in perfect peace, whose mind is stayed on Thee: because he trusteth in Thee" (Isa. 26:1-3). In these inspired words, the gospel prophet assures us that the gates into this "strong city" are thrown open to all those who keep the truth, and that *those who picture themselves* (see margin, v. 3) as being kept safely within God's appointed "walls and bulwarks" of "salvation" will be kept in "perfect peace." Again we read from Isaiah's pen: "Thou shalt call thy walls Salvation, and thy gates Praise. . . . The Lord shall be unto thee an everlasting light, and thy God thy glory" (Isa. 60:18-20). The Psalmist says: "Open to me the gates of righteousness: I will go into them, and I will praise the Lord: this gate of the Lord, into which the righteous shall enter. I will praise Thee: for Thou *art* become my salvation" (Ps. 118:19-21). "The name of the Lord is a *strong tower*: the righteous runneth into it, and is safe" (Prov. 18:10). "The Lord is my rock, and my *fortress*, and my *Deliverer* . . . He is my *shield* . . . my *high tower*, and my *refuge*, my *Saviour*; Thou savest me from violence. . . . He is *the tower of salvation*" (2 Sam. 22:2, 3, 51). See also Ps. 18:2; 144:2, etc.

This picture of an individual or of the church dwelling securely within the mighty walls of an impregnable fortress is carried over into the encouraging imagery of the book of Revelation, where the great struggle between the forces of good and evil is so graphically and so realistically portrayed that some, not discerning the moral purpose of the symbolism employed, think that a military war is therein depicted.

The best way to memorize is to reduce to a symbol that which we desire to commit to memory, and by the law of association that symbol brings to the mind all that is associated with it. Symbols present truths in the most arresting and most informative form. Mighty truths are thus condensed and made simple and clear. For this reason the Great Teacher presents the vital teachings of the Apocalypse in symbolic form.

The reader is urged to cultivate the symbol-picture of the soul as a fortress: when surrounded and assaulted by many enemies—pride, selfishness, envy, jealousy, greed, dark, negative thoughts, etc.—seeking to obtain an entrance into the citadel of the soul, the dark invader is repulsed and victory is won through King Jesus—the Light and Life-giver—dwelling within. To inculcate this teaching in the minds of His children, and to enable them to grasp these soul-stirring facts of salvation, is *the moral purpose* for which the Lord inspired John to present the *symbolic pictures* of the Apocalypse: *they present Christian realities.*

A widely-read author, who consistently applies the martial imagery of the Apocalypse as descriptive of the great controversy between Christ and Satan, employs the same Biblical imagery we have presented to teach that the *individual's* victory over sin depends upon the indwelling Christ.

"When *the soul* surrenders itself to Christ, a new power takes possession of the heart. A change is wrought which man can never accomplish for himself. It is a supernatural work, bringing a supernatural element into human nature. *The soul* that is yielded to Christ becomes *His own fortress*, which He holds in a revolted world, and He intends that no authority shall be known in it but His own. A soul thus kept in possession by the heavenly agencies is *impregnable to the assaults of Satan. . . .* The only defense against evil is *the indwelling of Christ in the heart* through faith in His righteousness" (*The Desire of Ages*, p. 324).

In another book, this writer employs the same imagery in describing the power of *the church* to withstand the assaults of her enemies:

"*The church* is God's agency for the proclamation of truth, . . . and if she is loyal to Him, obedient to all His commandments, there will *dwell within her* the excellency of divine grace. If she will be true to her allegiance, if she will honor the Lord God of

Israel, there is no power that can stand against her" (*The Acts of the Apostles*, p. 600).

Individuals and the church are likened to "a city that is set on an hill" (Matt. 5:14). The Christian church and individual believers are represented in the prophecy of Ezekiel (chaps. 40-48) as a temple built upon "a very high mountain." Jesus said: "Upon this rock [Himself, "the Rock of Ages"] I will build My church; and *the gates of hell shall not prevail against it*" (Matt. 16:18). The New Testament teaches that the church is now God's Zion, His city Jerusalem, and that prophecies concerning enemies being destroyed when attacking Jerusalem and God's people have their moral purpose in relation to the victory of each individual believer in Christ and of the church as a whole.

In the book of Revelation, the storm center of the ages is the city of Jerusalem, the name of which means "foundations of peace"; Jerusalem, the city of "the Prince of Peace." To correctly understand the Revelation, Jerusalem must be interpreted as the center of the battle between good and evil. In the Old Testament, Jerusalem was the center of national Israel, and many of Israel's national enemies came against Jerusalem—the city of "peace." Though foes were without, peace reigned within the city when Israel was faithful. In this we see typified the church as a whole, and also each individual. Through their allegiance to the God of Israel, the church and individual Christians become the center of attack by foes who are stirred to "war" against the Holy Son of God within. But, while spiritual enemies gather outside the walls of "the holy city" (Rev. 11:2, etc.), the heart is at peace with God.

Enemies of the people of God who literally gathered around and attacked ancient Israel's literal city of "peace" are brought into the spiritual imagery of the Revelation as types of the enemies who spiritually gather around to attack the spiritual city. The Revelation carries this *representation* through *until the end of the millennium*; then, all the resurrected literal enemies of ancient Israel and all the enemies of the church will *literally* gather around the *literal city* (Rev. 20:8, 9) in which reigns the visible Son of God, the Destroyer of the evil which makes "war" on Him and His people. In Joel 2:32, deliverance from the foes without the city is vouchsafed to "the remnant" within Jerusalem: "For *in mount Zion* and *in Jerusalem* shall be *deliverance*, as the Lord hath said, and in the remnant whom He shall call." As we have already seen, it is from this prophecy that Peter, in his Spirit-filled address, quotes on the day of Pentecost and applies it in connection with salvation through *King* Jesus, Who is "both *Lord* and Christ." Instances are given in the Old Testament where national Israel found deliverance within Jerusalem through the power of God (see 2 Kings 18:17-37; 19:1-37; Isa. 37:32-36, etc.). At the end of the millennium, when the enemies of God and of His people gather to attack "the camp of the saints," "and the beloved city" (Rev. 20:8, 9), they are destroyed through the almighty power of "the King of Righteousness,' the Lord Jesus Christ, Who reigns within.

All the proper names, places and designations of the Revelation are employed in a symbolical sense until the Revelator's description of the holy city—New Jerusalem—*at the end of the millennium.* Thus the Lord shows the principle to be employed in "rightly dividing" the Apocalypse and other parts of the Holy Scriptures. The millennium is the dividing line between the application of the spiritual and the application of the literal, just as the cross terminated the *literal, national, typical* system, and introduced the period of the *antitypical, spiritual, or church* application. The Revelation clearly reveals the *triple* application of the things of Israel, but as we have dealt with that theme in another book, we will not discuss it further here.

As the history of ancient Israel is applied in the New Testament as *types* or *symbols* depicting the experiences of the church, and as the church is represented as having taken the place of national Israel, *even to its geographical setting in Palestine*, so, in the Revelation the Lord has described the present-day experiences of His church in *symbolical terms.* Though buffeted by many foes, the church, "on the mount Sion" (Rev. 14:1, 20; Ezek. 40:2; 43:12; 47:1, etc.), as a mighty fortress, impregnable to the assaults of the enemy, will be "*more than conquerors through Him that loved us*" (Rom. 8:37). "Thanks be to God, which *giveth us the victory through our Lord Jesus Christ*" (1 Cor. 15:57).

The great controversy between the forces of good and evil over obedience to the Law of God will culminate in "the final conflict." To vividly portray this *spiritual* battle *is the moral purpose for which the graphic symbolic pictures have been given in the Revelation.*

ADDENDUM — A BRIEF OUTLINE

The belief that "Armageddon" will be a military conflict in Palestine is part of the Futuristic system which is based upon a literal application of the things of ancient Israel, in contrast to the New Testament spiritual application in relation to the church. The errors of Roman Catholicism are based upon the literal application of the things of national Israel. Protestant Futurists may not appreciate their interpretation of prophecy being coupled up with the errors of Roman Catholicism; but they have the same foundation. Futurism has been fostered by Roman Catholicism because of its potent force against true Protestantism.

Dr. H. G. Guinness, in his *Approaching End of the Age*, pages 100, 101, writes of the Futuristic view: "In its present form, however, it may be said to have originated, at the end of the sixteenth century, with Jesuit Ribera, who, moved like Alcasar, to relieve the Papacy from the stigma cast upon it by the Protestant interpretation, tried to do so by referring these to the distant *future. . . . For a considerable period this view was confined to Romanists* [italics mine], and was refuted by several masterly Protestant works."

The Roman Catholic Church justifies its ornate buildings and ritual, etc., by pointing to the literal things of ancient Israel (see their *Question Box*, pp. 187-189; *Keenan's Catechism*, pp. 193-212, etc.).

The following brief outline is intended to convey "much in little," and to provoke the reader to study further into the fundamental principles of interpretation.

"THE MYSTERY OF GODLINESS" (1 Tim. 3:16)	"THE MYSTERY OF INIQUITY" (2 Thess. 2:7)
SPIRITUAL APPLICATION OF THE THINGS OF ISRAEL	LITERAL APPLICATION OF THE THINGS OF ISRAEL
Temple—Church (1 Cor. 3:16; Ephes. 2:21).	Temple.
Priests—on earth, all believers (1 Peter 2:9).	Priests.
Incense—prayer (Ps. 141:2; Rev. 5:8).	Incense.
Cross—daily self-denial (Luke 9:23).	Cross.
Light in Temple—Bible (Ps. 119:105; 2 Cor. 4:4, etc.).	Candles.
Bread—Word of God (John 6:27-68).	Wafer-mass.
Water—Holy Spirit working through Word of God (Tit. 3:5; Eph. 5:26).	"Holy" water.
Fire in which dross is burned:— 1) Work of Holy Spirit (Matt. 3:11; Isa. 4:4; 1 Pet. 1:7; 4:12). 2) Obedience to truth purifies (1 Pet. 1:22).	Purgatory.
KING—CHRIST—INVISIBLE (1 Tim. 1:17).	Pope—visible head.
Holy Spirit—Invisible Representative (John 14:17).	Supposed Representative of Christ.
Throne in each heart (Rom. 5:17-21).	Visible Throne in Rome (Rev. 16:10; 17:18).
Kingdom—Spiritual. Those delivered from sin (Col. 1:13).	Kingdom—literal: Political power.
War—Spiritual war; worldwide conflict. "War a good warfare" (1 Tim. 1:18). "Fight the good fight of faith" (1 Tim. 6:12).	War—Military conflict in Palestine. Fight—Military conflict in Palestine.
Peace— spiritual peace—God and soul (New Testament about 110 times, Paul about 52 times).	Peace—Military "peace."
Enemies—"Gentiles," "Heathen"; those who are not Israelites (Eph. 2:11, 12; Rev. 11:2) in any part of the world.	"Heathen," "Gentiles"—Literal nations east of Palestine.
Israel—Church in all the world (Gal. 6:16; Rev. 7:1-4, etc.).	"Israel"—A few literal Jews in Palestine.
Israel attacked by enemies—Spiritual enemies (Ezek. 38, 39; Joel 3; Zech. 14; Rev. 14:1, 20; 16:12-16; 17:14, etc.).	Israel attacked by enemies— Literal nations to literally attack literal Jews in Palestine.

Teaches that Anti-Christ is a spiritual leader: A counterfeit *church* which makes "war with the saints" (Rev. 13:7).	Teaches that Anti-Christ is a military leader; a person to dominate literal Jews in Palestine.
Symbolic Time (Dan. 7:25; Rev. 11:2; 12:6, 12; 13:5). Affecting the church.	Literal Time (3½ literal years); affecting literal Jews in Palestine.